RESEARCH DISCUSSION SERIES NO. 17

EDUCATIONAL REFORMS AND GENDER EQUALITY IN SCHOOLS

Madeleine Arnot, *Department of Education, University of Cambridge*
Miriam David, *Social Sciences Research Centre, South Bank University*
Gaby Weiner, *School of Education, South Bank University*

EQUAL OPPORTUNITIES COMMISSION

ISBN 1 870358 54 6

EOC RESEARCH DISCUSSION SERIES

The EOC Research Discussion Series provides a channel for the dissemination of reviews of research and the secondary analysis of data carried out by Research Unit staff or externally commissioned research workers.

The views expressed in this report are those of the authors and do not necessarily represent the views of the Commission. The Commission is publishing the report as a contribution to discussion and debate.

The EOC Research Discussion Series is available from:
The Publications Unit
EOC
Overseas House
Quay Street
Manchester
M3 3HN

Research Unit
Equal Opportunities Commission
Overseas House
Quay Street
Manchester M3 3HN

Also in London, Cardiff and Glasgow

CONTENTS

TABLES AND FIGURES

FIGURES

ABBREVIATIONS AND ACRONYMS

List of abbreviations and acronyms used in the report

A-LEVEL	GCE Advanced Level
ACAC	Curriculum and Assessment Authority for Wales
ALIS	A-Level Information System
APU	Assessment of Performance Unit
AS-LEVEL	Advanced Scholarship Examination
BTEC	Business and Technological Education Council
CCW	Curriculum Council for Wales
CDT	Craft, Design and Technology
CEO	Chief Education Officer
CGLI	City and Guilds London Institute
CPVE	Certificate of Pre-Vocational Education
CSE	Certificate of Secondary Education
CTC	City Technology College
DES	Department of Education and Science
DfE	Department for Education
ED	Department of Employment
EO	Equal Opportunities
EOC	Equal Opportunities Commission
ERA	Education Reform Act (1988)
FAS	Funding Agency for Schools
FE	Further Education
FT	Foundation Target
GCE	General Certificate of Education
GCSE	General Certificate of Secondary Education
GEST	Grants for Educational Support and Training
GM(S)	Grant Maintained (Schools)
GNVQ	General National Vocational Qualification
HMI	Her Majesty's Inspectors of Schools
HNC	Higher National Certificate
HND	Higher National Diploma

ILEA	Inner London Education Authority
INSET	In-service education or training for school staff
KS1-4	Key Stages 1-4 in the National Curriculum
LEA	Local Education Authority
LMS	Local Management of Schools
MFL	Modern Foreign Language
NACETT	National Advisory Council for Education and Training Targets
NCC	National Curriculum Council
NETT	National Education and Training Target
NISVQ	National Information System for Vocational Qualifications
NUT	National Union of Teachers
NVQ	National Vocational Qualification
OFSTED	Office for Standards in Education
OHMCI	Office of Her Majesty's Chief Inspector (Welsh 'OFSTED')
O-LEVEL	GCE Ordinary Level
ONC	Ordinary National Certificate
PE	Physical Education
PSE	Personal and Social Education
QLFS	Quarterly Labour Force Survey
RSA	Royal Society of Arts
SAT	Standard Attainment Target or Task
SCAA	Schools Curriculum and Assessment Authority
SEAC	Schools Examination and Assessment Council for England and Wales
TODW	Take Our Daughters to Work initiative
TTA	Teacher Training Agency
TVEI	Technical and Vocational Education Initiative
UK	United Kingdom
VA	Value-Added

ACKNOWLEDGEMENTS

A team of researchers supported the project: at Cambridge University, Elizabeth Gray and Dr. Charles Newbould of the Oxford and Cambridge Schools Examination Board were particularly important in the development of the analyses of examination results for GCSE and A-levels and Debbie Mills provided secretarial assistance; at South Bank University, Dr. Jonathan Tritter and Laura Hart contributed to the development and analysis of the questionnaires and Jackie Davies and Sally Mitchell made major inputs into the case-studies. Additionally at South Bank, Beverley Goring, Joshua Berle, Mehul Kotecha, Toby Reiner and Ian Zeider helped with the initial administration and distribution of the questionnaires; and Jennifer Siegel produced the final report. The Welsh part of the project was coordinated by Dr. Sara Delamont of the University of Wales College at Cardiff; and valuable contributions to the case-studies were provided by Dr. Jane Salisbury.

We are particularly grateful to our co-researchers for their help and support in developing this complex research study. We also thank everyone to whom we spoke or corresponded with in LEAs, schools and various educational agencies and teacher unions for their cooperation and support for the project. Our thanks also go to Surrey County Council, BTEC and Alan Felstead et al. for permission to use their research data. Finally, we would like to thank the EOC for providing us with the opportunity to undertake so fascinating a study; in particular Sue Arthur (now at the Policy Studies Institute), Lorraine Fletcher, Liz Speed, Anne Madden and Ed Puttick.

Madeleine Arnot
Miriam David
Gaby Weiner

FOREWORD

Education is a prime concern for the EOC. The experiences and choices of young people at school have lifelong effects in their opportunities and economic well being. The Commission is committed to seeking improved gender equality on education and has identified education as a key focus in its 1995-1999 Corporate Plan for priority work.

This research has shown that there have been positive developments at a national and local level - improvements in the delivery of equal opportunities and in outcomes for girls and boys. However, concerns remain about the level of support for teachers working on gender issues in the classroom.

Boys and girls have different strengths and weaknesses which must be tackled. Girls have become more successful in GCSE examinations, whilst boys are better in vocational qualifications. And more work is needed to address the underachievement of boys in schools.

Removing traditional attitudes and subject choices will help everyone to reach their full potential. The current polarisation of subject choices for girls and boys and their different work aspirations leads to the job segregation and pay differential for men and women in later life. And with significant changes in the workplace and the need for greater skill and flexibility in the workforce, it is now even more important that all young people are encouraged to gain a wider range of qualifications.

The findings of this research highlight recent developments which have resulted in positive changes in schools. The publication of increased data in the form of SAT results means that we are now able to recognise differences in achievements of girls and boys from 7 onwards - and therefore to do something about improving performance where necessary. The EOC is encouraging the setting of equality targets in schools to address differential achievements at all stages and for all subjects.

TVEI is widely acknowledged as an initiative which has had a tremendous impact on the development of equality in technical and vocational subjects and in gender equality generally in schools. This impetus must be maintained and developed through new curriculum initiatives now funding for TVEI has ceased.

The research also shows that the OFSTED Inspection, with its equal opportunities requirements, has been a catalyst for equal opportunities work in schools and provides a mechanism for the delivery of gender work on a wider and more systematic basis than has previously been required.

The Commission will use this research in its work with national policy makers and local practitioners to highlight the key role which gender plays in educational achievement and post-school destinations and to encourage gender work as an integral and essential part of improving the quality of education in our schools and the opportunities for all young people.

EXECUTIVE SUMMARY

INTRODUCTION

This research report considers educational reforms and gender equality in schools in England and Wales in the period 1984-1994. In particular, it assesses whether the various educational changes of the late 1980s and early 1990s have strengthened or interrupted previous trends and/or generated new trends towards greater gender equality.

The project started in March 1994 and lasted for a year. It was directed jointly by Cambridge University and South Bank University, with the Welsh research team based at Cardiff University.

The point at which the research was carried out followed, first, a period of equal opportunities activity in education which reached its height in the mid 1980s, in which local education authorities took a major role: and secondly, a period of considerable educational change instigated by government reforms which encouraged greater central control over schools, as well as choice, competition and the introduction of educational markets, through self managing schools and new school provision.

THE AIMS OF THE PROJECT

- To assess national patterns of gender equality in primary and secondary education in England and Wales over the period 1984-94;

- to elicit the views of primary and secondary schools in England and Wales on the impact of recent educational changes as they have affected gender equality;

- to elicit the views of LEAs on the impact of recent educational changes on the promotion of gender equality in schools;

- to explore any further or unanticipated gender issues that have emerged for schools and LEAs;

- to identify school and LEA policies and strategies for promoting gender equality in schools and in adult life.

PROJECT METHODOLOGY

Three different approaches to data collection and analysis were used in the study, in order to describe and explain the various patterns and trends in gender equality in schools over the last decade. The main research approaches used were:

i)   Analysis of statistics on examination entry and performance data for the period 1984-1994.

ii)   Postal surveys of:
   - national samples of primary and secondary maintained and grant maintained schools (including all CTCs) in England and Wales;
   - all LEAs in England and Wales.

iii)   Case studies of equal opportunities policy and practice in seven selected LEAs in England and Wales.

THE POLICY CONTEXT

Education in England and Wales has experienced major policy changes over the last decade, either specifically directed towards the reform of education or towards other parts of the public sector, which have nevertheless impacted on education.   Some changes are particular to Wales. The reforms with which the project has been particularly concerned include:

- The New Training Initiative (1981) and consequent development of pre-vocational courses;

- Changes in examinations (for 16 and 18 year olds), particularly the replacement of O-Level and CSE with GCSE (first introduced in 1985);

- The Education Act (1986);

- The Education Reform Act (ERA) (1988);

- The introduction of the Citizen's Charter (1991) and the Parent's Charter *You and Your Child's Education*;

- The Education (Schools) Act (1992) which included the introduction of a new system of regular statutory inspections for schools conducted by members of OFSTED;

- The Education Act (1993).

Few of the new policies were framed or developed with equal opportunities in mind. There has been therefore little explicit reference to gender equality, although implicit policy intentions may have been to improve equality of opportunity.

During this period, understanding and definitions of the concept of equal opportunities have also undergone substantial change, whether between the sexes or for other social groups. The early 1980s saw an accelerating interest in gender issues in public debates - through the media as well as through the growth of teacher and LEA led policy initiatives and research. Changes in the climate of opinion thus also provide a context for educational changes.

THE FRAMEWORK FOR ANALYSIS

The Gender Gap

The concept of the *gender gap* was used to discuss the ways in which different patterns of (a) examination entry and (b) examination performance had changed in the period under study. The gender gap denotes the measure of difference between the sexes in relation to the proportion of the male and female age cohort who entered for a particular subject and the proportion of those who achieved either A-C grades at GCSE or A/B grades at A-level.

The project also distinguished between curriculum and organisation reforms as follows:

Curricular Reforms

Developments and changes in the school curriculum and in vocational education; assessment and related forms of testing and examinations; monitoring of school performance; tables of school examinations and results.

Organisational Reforms

Developments and changes in the organisation and control of schools; shifts from LEA provision to greater diversity of school type, with open enrolment, GMS and CTCs: increased power of school governing bodies.

GENDER AND ACHIEVEMENT PATTERNS (1984 - 1994)

General

- Early SATs data suggest that gender patterns are being shaped at an early age - girls at Key Stages 1 and 2 appear to be achieving higher performances than boys, particularly in English; more boys are scoring at the extremes of the grading scheme particularly in Mathematics and Science, and are underachieving in English at ages 7 and 11.

- Trends in relation to gender at GCSE and A-level established before the reforms in terms of improving male and female entry and performance have continued throughout the period.

- Sex stereotyping in the selection of vocational courses remains a continuing feature of vocational education, with young men and women choosing to study for different occupational qualifications.

- There has been a considerable rise in achievement of all post compulsory qualifications, especially among young women. Data on school leavers suggest that there are national, regional, ethnic and social differences in gender patterns.

- Data on entry and performance in vocational education are patchy and incomplete, so identification of trends and patterns has proved difficult to determine.

- The gender gap in favour of men is much greater for vocational qualifications than for academic qualifications. Men under the age of 21 retain their advantage overall in acquiring vocational qualifications and course choices appear to follow traditional gendered (occupational) lines.

GCSE Patterns

- There has been a considerable increase in GCSE entry with the entry gender gap closing substantially for most subjects, leaving only Chemistry, Economics (both favouring male students) and Social Studies (favouring female students) with increasingly unequal take up.

- Female students, in particular, have been increasing their entry into the full range of subjects, including the traditionally 'male' Sciences, Computer Studies and Mathematics.

- Male students have increasingly entered the Arts and Modern Foreign Languages, thus reducing the gender entry gap in those subjects.

- Female students have been improving their performance markedly in relation to GCSE entry (especially in those subjects with higher male entries), whereas male students have not shown similar improvements in their examination performances in the period. They have been achieving relatively less well in English, the Arts, Humanities, Modern Foreign, Languages and Technology.

- In 1994, single sex girls' schools produced higher overall grades (e.g. 5 GCSEs with grades A-C) than single sex boys' schools, irrespective of school type; in 6 out of 7 categories of schools, girls' schools achieved proportionately the highest performances.

A-Level Patterns

- In terms of entry patterns, both the gender gap in favour of male students in most of the Sciences and the gender gap in favour of female students in the Humanities and Arts remain, although the latter is now decreasing.

- Young men have been increasing their entry advantage in subjects such as Physics, Technology, Computer Studies, Economics and Geography, maintaining their advantage in entry to Chemistry and Mathematics and improving their take up of 'female' subjects such as English and Modern Foreign Languages.

- Young men continue to achieve higher performances in relation to their entry than young women in nearly all subjects (especially in Mathematics, Chemistry, Technology, History and even in English and Modern Foreign Languages where they are in the minority), but this advantage is gradually being reduced.

- There has been a marked improvement in female performance at A-level over the period in almost all subject areas. Young women are now gaining higher performances in relation to their entry than male students in Biology, Social Studies, Art and Design, and are closing the gap in performance even in those A-level subjects in which they are proportionately fewer (e.g. Physics, Mathematics).

Vocational Qualifications

- Recent research suggests that young women have higher course completion rates for vocational courses such as BTEC, especially in those boards where female candidates predominate.

- Gender differences in vocational qualifications appear to be ethnically based, with some groups of young women being more successful than young men in the same minority ethnic group (e.g. Indian origin), although in most other groups the reverse is true.

- Students continue to choose vocational courses (e.g. BTEC) according to conventional sex-stereotypes, with young women opting, for example, for courses in Business and Commerce, Hairdressing and Beauty, Caring Services (e.g. Nursery Nursing) and Science (e.g. dental assisting). Young men continue to opt for courses in Engineering and Construction and mainstream Science subjects (e.g. Physics, Chemistry).

- Some changes in student course choice have begun to emerge in, for example, male students choosing Business and Finance BTEC courses.

- Female students appear less likely than male students to achieve higher NVQ levels 2 and 3 through traditional vocational courses, but are more likely to take and obtain higher levels of achievement in new vocational courses (GNVQs, NVQs).

EQUAL OPPORTUNITIES POLICY- MAKING

- Most (two thirds) schools and LEAs have specialist equal opportunities policies; 98 per cent of LEAs and 81 per cent of primary and 93 per cent of secondary schools reported having an equal opportunities policy which included gender. Eighty three per cent of these school policies were produced after the 1988 Education Reform Act.

- School and LEA equal opportunities policies on gender tend to focus on curriculum practice and employment concerns rather than on pupil or student performance or on parents. A quarter of LEAs policies do not apply to pupils and only two out of five policies include parents.

- The main impetus for the development of equal opportunities policies and practices has come from LEAs and headteachers in the case of primary schools, and from LEAs, headteachers, committed teachers and TVEI in the case of secondary schools.

- Approximately half of English and two thirds of Welsh LEAs reported an increased role in the development of gender equality in the primary sector since the reforms. Neither parents nor parent governors are reported to have played an active role in the development of equal opportunity policy making.

- Approximately half of the secondary schools in the project reported having a designated coordinator of post of responsibility for equal opportunities (including gender). In primary schools such posts are rarer.

- Equality issues are not viewed as a high priority by most schools and LEAs. Less than 10 per cent gave gender issues a high priority; approximately 30 per cent claimed to be 'moderately interested' or 'actively involved' in developing equal opportunities policies.

- Primary schools are less likely to have policies on equal opportunities and to see equal opportunities as integral to their practice rather than as a discrete priority.

- Wide variation amongst schools and LEAs exists in the awareness and applications of gender issues, in the interpretation of equal opportunities and in trends in student performance.

LEA - SCHOOL RELATIONS
- The educational reforms, particularly local management of school (LMS), have altered LEA-school relations, shifting responsibility for equal opportunities from LEAs to individual schools. The impact of this shift is differentially felt, depending on existing LEA-school relations and history of policy development on equality issues.

- LEAs reported low levels of involvement in introducing curriculum reforms in schools and in influencing, particularly, secondary school policies and practices. They claimed to have been a major factor in supporting equal opportunities in schools through provision of specialist services, monitoring and training functions and advisory support. This is not a view shared by schools which typically report low levels of LEA support for equal opportunities work.

- Fewer than one fifth of primary and secondary schools in England and Wales reported receiving support on equal opportunities issues from the LEA; less than one per cent claimed to be receiving support through coordinated school networks or financial assistance.

- Seventy per cent of primary and secondary schools claimed not to have had LEA-provided equal opportunities training for senior managers, classroom teachers or careers teachers. Only a third of school governing bodies were reported to be taking responsibility for providing training and for monitoring gender performance in schools.

- Governor training on equal opportunities was patchy with 85 per cent of the LEAs reporting provision; however only a minority (less than 4 out of 10) of schools recorded receiving such support.

PERSPECTIVES ON EDUCATIONAL REFORMS

- Changes to the curriculum and examinations (e.g. TVEI, GCSE, National Curriculum, SATs) are seen largely to have a positive impact on promoting equal opportunities, particularly in secondary schools.

- TVEI was reported to have had a positive (or even a very positive) effect on equal opportunities by 87 per cent of secondary schools; similarly 72 per cent saw positive effects of GCSE.

- Reforms concerning the monitoring of performance and standards, and new systems of school inspections using equal opportunities criteria have tended to focus attention on the reduction of gender difference; two thirds of LEAs claimed that OFSTED had raised the profile of equal opportunities.

- Administrative and organisational reforms, provisions to support greater parental choice, and financial changes have been seen by LEAs as having a largely negative effect on gender equality. These include the introduction of LMS, GMS, CTCs, representing a parallel loss of power of LEAs which in some instances were actively engaged with promoting greater gender equality.

- CTCs appear to want to be associated with equal opportunities policies and have better facilities for Science and Technology. However, there are no early indicators of changed gender patterns in subject choice or in take-up of scientific or technological careers.

- Gender is perceived as having moved *downwards* in the policy agenda particularly in LEAs with a greater commitment to equal opportunities. Small shifts *upwards* are discerned, post 1988, in other schools and LEAs which for the first time have been required to address gender issues in their reporting and evaluation procedures.

CHANGING GENDER CULTURES

- Gender issues are now being framed within the new language of schooling arising out of the post-reform era. Some schools have brought gender issues into line with concerns about performance, standards and value-added policies; others have focused on broader based and more inclusive concepts of entitlement and effective citizenship. The language of equal opportunities policy-making has, to some extent, adapted to and become part of the new mainstream culture of schools.

- Pupils' perception of gender issues, across a range of ages and social groups and localities, were seen as more open and more sensitive to changing cultural expectations and/or changes in the labour market. For example, girls and young women appeared more confident and positive about their future working lives and opportunities. Boys and young men also seemed aware of gender debates about women's working lives. Nevertheless, occupational choices for both sexes appear to remain conventional and stereotyped.

- Schools and LEAs were found to be shaped largely by the culture of male management (in the staffing, and chairs of governing bodies), with little obvious strategic planning in relation to gender inequalities in the teaching profession.

xvii

- New areas of concern have emerged such as boys' under-achievement. This is beginning to be perceived as a major gender issue in schools, although there is little evidence of strong parental concern for gender issues.

- Initiatives on equal opportunities have been developed in certain LEAs and schools in England and Wales, although most have been 'in house' and do not appear to have been widely publicised or discussed. Many of these initiatives specifically address the post reform context (e.g. OFSTED inspections, valued added policies, monitoring of performance, governor training, women in management), fusing considerations of social justice with those arising out of more recent concerns about performance standards.

POLICY IMPLICATIONS

Data Collection

- The introduction of comprehensive and uniform monitoring of achievement levels by gender (as well as for other social categories) has revealed the value of such measures in identifying educational and occupational trends and patterns for male and female students.

- The data however are not currently collected in a form which allows for national evaluation on gender equality. The examination mapping exercise undertaken for the project reveals the gaps, inadequacies and limitations of official data sources, for different qualifications over the ten year period of study. This has consequently drawn attention to the need for a regular and routine national system of data collection on examination performance by gender using consistent base-lines and age cohorts.

- Similarly the patterns of choice and performance in vocational education identified by the project suggest the importance of monitoring and evaluating the new framework of vocational qualifications in terms of gender.

- Further research is needed on how gender issues are experienced and integrated into school practice. In-depth studies have been important in identifying variety and diversity of provision and approach.

Curriculum Issues

The analysis of pupil performance has identified a number of curriculum concerns. For example:

- the continuing narrowed aspirations of girls and young women when selecting subject options and future occupational possibilities, despite their improved performance, relative to boys, in examinations;

- the relative underachievement of boys and young men in English, Modern Foreign Languages and the Humanities in schooling up to KS4, in contrast to their higher achievement at A-levels and in acquiring higher level vocational qualifications;

- the relative failure of young women to take up Mathematics and the Sciences post 16;

- the reintroduction of choice in subjects such as Technology, (resourcing questions in single sex schools) and the possible effects of post Dearing reforms on examination entry and performance trends.

Policy Development

The positive identification of strong central direction with increased gender awareness (e.g. OFSTED equal opportunities criteria, TVEI equal opportunities requirements, initiatives on careers' guidance) suggests that equality initiatives that demand targets and accountability are likely to be more effective than those mainly dependent on individual commitment or voluntary effort.

Gaps in equal opportunities support are noticeable despite increased development of equal opportunities policies. These include **lack** of:

- governor training and classroom focused INSET;
- awareness and involvement of parents and parent governors;
- awareness among headteachers and classroom teachers (particularly at primary level) of the range of policy and curriculum strategies available;
- coordinated specialist resource centres, and libraries; and,
- coordinated equal opportunities networks and advisory expertise.

CONCLUDING POINTS

Cultural, demographic and labour market changes have influenced the way students and teachers think about the schooling of girls and boys, such that most now consider girls' education to be equally important. High scoring female students are proving attractive to schools in the competitive climate of the 1990s, and it is poorly behaved and low achieving boys up to 16 who appear to be the subjects of greatest concern.

The research revealed a mixed picture of beneficial procedures and policies arising from some of the reforms, pockets of thoughtful and knowledgeable practice from committed individuals and groups, but overall, no infrastructure for the delivery of equal opportunities on a wider and more systematic basis.

There remain wide areas of concern about the impact of social class and minority ethnic origins on male and female student achievement and the extent and depth of understanding and perception of gender issues in schools. If the shifts towards greater gender equality identified by the project are to continue, efforts need to be made to explore those issues which were not addressed by the project, to create a sound infrastructure for the delivery of equal educational opportunities and to build upon the commitment of the many involved in education to provide genuinely better opportunities for future generations of female and male citizens.

1   INTRODUCTION

This research report[1] considers educational reforms and gender equality in schools in England and Wales for the period 1984 to 1994. In particular, it assesses in what ways the various educational reforms of the late 1980s and early 1990s have strengthened or interrupted previous patterns and/or generated new trends.

The project started in March 1994 and lasted for a year. It was directed jointly by Cambridge University and South Bank University, with a Welsh research team based at Cardiff University.

1.1   AIMS OF THE PROJECT

- To assess national patterns of gender equality in primary and secondary education in England and Wales over the period 1984-94.

- To elicit the views of primary and secondary schools in England and Wales about the impact of recent educational changes as they have affected gender equality.

- To elicit the views of Local Education Authorities (LEAs) about the impact of recent educational changes on the promotion of gender equality in schools.

- To explore any further or unanticipated gender issues that have emerged for schools and LEAs.

- To identify school and LEA policies and strategies for promoting gender equality in schools and in adult life.

---

[1]   A separate report is available for Wales which includes additional data collection carried out at a later stage than the main project (Salisbury 1996)

1

1.2   PROJECT METHODOLOGY

Three different approaches to data collection and analysis were used in the study, in order to describe and explain the various patterns and trends in gender equality in schools over the last decade. The main research approaches used were:

- Analysis of statistics on examination and performance data for the period 1984-1994.

- Postal surveys of:

  - National samples of primary and secondary maintained schools (including all City Technology Colleges (CTCs)) in England and Wales.
  - All LEAs in England and Wales.

- Case studies of equal opportunities policy and practice in seven selected LEAs in England and Wales.

Analysis of Trends in Examination Entry and Performance

By examining trends in examination entry and performance, the main aim of the mapping exercise was to demonstrate if and how the *gender gap* between male and female subject choice and performance for various subjects and levels has changed over the ten-year period. Considerable effort was thus expended by the research team on identifying an appropriate method of mapping such trends in examinations, an exercise which proved problematic because of the various changes in examination and assessment over the period and also because of the unsystematic, patchy and variable ways in which examination data had been kept over the years.

For these reasons and also because of the limited scale of the project, it was decided to focus primarily on subject and course choice and performance data relating to academic and vocational pathways, limiting data collection to schools - although the same subjects and examinations may be studied at Further Education (FE) colleges etc.

Attempts to map trends were further frustrated by changes in methods of data collection over the decade in question. Indeed, the nature of the curriculum reforms particularly has led to changes in the data held, for example, on subject and course titles, clusters of subjects and vocational qualifications, and for the scales used; for example, in 1994 for the first time the General Certificate of Secondary Education (GCSE) had a starred 'A' category.

Another problem for the mapping exercise was the varied geographical constituency of published data. Some refer to England only, some include Wales (often not separately identified), others combine data from England, Wales and Northern Ireland; and it is sometimes not possible to untangle (or disaggregate) national patterns. Some analyses of examination data focus on individuals, and others focus on curriculum subjects, age or study cohorts. (Appendix A on project methodology contains a more detailed discussion of the limitations of official data sources.)

Thus for the purposes of mapping trends, it was decided to select four 'snapshot' years for analysis (1985, 1988, 1991 and 1994). The two main examination periods for students which take place at the end of year 11 (GCSE) and Year 13 (A-level) were used as the key stages in the trend analysis. Vocational subjects were considered separately as patterns of take-up and study tend to be more diverse.

Moreover, because presenting findings on examinations in the form of absolute numbers (or as raw scores) does not take into account changes in cohort sizes and in the student population, it was decided rather to present findings relative to specific year cohorts and separately for each sex. Thus, entry and performance statistics were indexed for each subject using as a base-line an estimate of the age cohort size for each sex for the year in question.

For the Year 11 cohort, the total number of candidates was assumed to be those taking GCSE English (Language) - very few Year 11 students, in fact, do not take this subject (roughly 3 per cent). Thus the index base of 100 (per cent) for males used for the project was the number of male students taking English in a particular year. A similar index base was used to ascertain the number of female students in any one year.

For Year 13 school students, no similar proxy exists for the age cohort size, since take-up of subjects is more diverse and many adults take A-levels, for example, in Further and Adult Education institutions. However, it is generally assumed that school students form 70 per cent of the A-level cohort in any one year. Thus the index base used for Year 13 was 70 per cent of the number of female and male students respectively who took one or more A-levels in any one year. Hence, calculations were made on the basis of the numbers of male and female school students studying specific subjects as a percentage (70 per cent) of the overall entry for those subjects. (See Appendix A for a more detailed discussion of this.)

Questionnaire Surveys of LEAs, and Primary and Secondary Schools

This part of the research had three main aims:

a. to explore the situation regarding gender equality in 1994, as perceived by maintained primary and secondary schools in England and Wales;

b. to compare and contrast the year 1984 with the year 1994 regarding gender equality and also to see how shifts over time have been perceived by schools and LEAs in England and Wales;

c. to elicit the views of schools and LEAs on the impact of the educational reforms and social changes relating to gender in/equality in schools.

Three separate but linked surveys were conducted: one survey each of a sample of maintained primary and secondary schools in England and Wales, and a third survey of all LEAs in England and Wales.

It was decided to include all middle schools and CTCs (of which there were 15) and some sixth form colleges in the school surveys, but to exclude designated special schools and the independent sector. In the absence of a database which covered the whole range of schools in England and Wales, the Schools Government Publishing Company drew up a national sampling frame based upon data for maintained schools for 1993-94. The samples were thus based on one in 20 primary schools and one in four secondary schools (and all CTCs) in England and Wales.

The following number of questionnaires were sent to LEAs and schools:

England

Secondary Schools	853	(including 152 grant maintained (GM))
CTCs	15	
Primary Schools	961	(including 18 GM)
LEAs	112	

Wales (Translated into Welsh for Welsh Medium Schools, English language copy also
provided)

Secondary Schools	58	(3 GM)
Primary Schools	85	(no GM)
LEAs	8	

The response rate overall to the surveys was low for a variety of reasons including factors
external to the project. (See Appendix A for a more detailed discussion of this.) This means,
therefore, that questionnaire findings need to be taken as an indication rather than a confirmation
of patterns and trends. The survey response rate was as follows:

England

Secondary Schools	214	(26%)
CTCs	9	(60%)
Primary Schools	359	(37%)
LEAs	49	(44%)

Wales

Secondary Schools	12	(21%)
Primary Schools	31	(36%)
LEAs	3	(38%)

The questionnaires were divided into four sections (five for secondary schools) with an additional
introductory section requesting information about the individuals completing the questionnaire.
The sections were:

- Policies on Equal Opportunities
- Structure of School/LEA
- Curriculum Menu (for secondary schools only)
- Education and Related Reforms
- Perceptions of Change

Case Studies of Equal Opportunities Policy and Practice in Selected LEAs
The aim of the case studies was to seek illumination, through focused in-depth study, of how
gender and equal opportunities policy-making were being experienced in individual schools and

in specific LEAs. The case study approach is multi-method yet focuses on an instance - in this case gender equality policy-making as experienced in chosen LEAs - and is frequently used to investigate and explain patterns and/or findings generated by other research methods. Case studies were therefore included as a supplement and illumination of the patterns and trends emerging from other parts of the project.

The unit chosen for each case study was that of the LEA area, and the focus of each study was the perceived impact of the education reforms on gender equality in that area. The precise nature of each study was negotiated to address local priorities as well as meeting the demands of the project.

A variety of forms of data collection was used: *interviews*, for example with LEA officers and advisors; Office for Standards in Education (OFSTED) inspectors[2]; Technical and Vocational Education Initiative (TVEI), curriculum and equal opportunities coordinators; headteachers; school staff and pupils/students; *observation* of classroom and workshop sessions, and of meetings, committees and working parts; and *documentation analysis* for example, of school prospectuses, LEA statistical information, OFSTED reports and written equal opportunities policies and documentation.

The aim of this part of the project was to explore the interconnection between local context and national policy-making through seven case studies (six in England and one in Wales) chosen to illustrate the variety of local contexts through which national policy is necessarily mediated. Thus information was sought on:

- development of equal opportunities policy at school and local level;
- gender patterns in school provision and pupil/student achievement;
- influences of the educational reforms on male and female education; and
- influences of the educational reforms on LEA support for school initiatives on gender equality.

Case study LEAs were selected on the basis of differing socio-economic context, range and diversity of school provision. The intention was to include LEAs representing a range of schools (e.g. denominational, secular, single-sex, coeducational, comprehensive, selective, GM, and

---

[2] OHMCI is the Welsh Office responsible for inspections and has a similar function to OFSTED. Throughout the report, unless otherwise stated, when OFSTED is mentioned, OHMCI is also included.

CTC); some with long histories of equal opportunities policy development and others with less evident experience in this area; and having different political affiliations and educational agendas. The case studies, with suitably descriptive pseudonyms, are as follows:

Shires LEA:

A large and predominantly white rural authority in the south of England, with a high percentage of GM schools and a low level of involvement in equal opportunities.

North West LEA:

Urban, with a high minority ethnic population, high proportion of church schools, declining population and high levels of inner-city disadvantage.

Home Counties LEA:

Located in a wealthy commuter belt, with a reputation of high achievement in school examinations, and a history of entrepreneurial initiatives including several on equal opportunities.

Midlands LEA:

Mainly urban, with concentrations of minority ethnic groups in some areas and a record of commitment to, and policy-making on, equal opportunities.

North East LEA:

A mix of rural and urban areas, mainly white, but with a small Asian community and with a past history of equal opportunities development.

London LEA:

Spanning the inner and outer city, with a large minority ethnic population and with a past history (when in ILEA) of policy awareness of equal opportunities.

Welsh LEA:

A mix of urban and rural communities with a small minority ethnic population, and with some past involvement in equal opportunities.

Case study LEAs were asked to identify schools and particular local initiatives and concerns, which might be of interest to the project. LEAs supported the project enthusiastically offering help with arranging school visits and providing local documentation. Research contracts (see Appendix A) were negotiated with each LEA (and school where appropriate) to confirm permission for the project to work in the authority and to protect confidentiality and anonymity of the individuals and schools who agreed to participate.

A range of primary and secondary schools were selected in each LEA, located variously in villages and small towns, inner and outer city areas, and covering diverse areas, for example, those with traditional working-class patterns of employment, with new service industries, and in the multiracial inner city and wealthy commuter belts. Some schools in the case studies were at the top of national school performance tables for GCSE and others were at the lower end.

1.3   STRUCTURE OF THE REPORT

Findings from the different parts of the project are integrated throughout the report; however, certain chapters concentrate on one specific aspect of the research. Thus, this chapter (one) provides a brief background to the project and some information on the research methods adopted for the project. Chapter 2 focuses on the educational policy context which provides the backdrop to the research study. In particular, it discusses the range of curriculum, assessment and organisational reforms, and reviews the developments in gender and equal opportunities policy-making prior to the research study. The next two chapters (three and four) present findings from the survey of examination data (at 16 plus and 18 plus) over a ten year time frame, and Chapter 5 explores the changing relationships between schools and LEAs as a consequence of the reforms, and what this has meant for gender equality in schools. Chapter 6 focuses on specific educational reforms and their respective impact on patterns of achievement and on equality perspectives whilst Chapter 7 considers the extent to which cultural as well as educational changes have brought about a changed culture with respect to gender equality in schools. The final chapter draws together the various project themes and findings in order to offer policy and practice implications for policy-makers and schools. A methodology appendix (Appendix A) is included which provides details of the research approaches adopted for the project, and some discussion about the complexity of mapping performance trends and of researching gender issues.

2   THE POLICY CONTEXT

Education in England and Wales has experienced major policy changes over the last decade. This is the consequence of central government policy, either specifically directed towards the reform of education or towards other parts of the public sector which have nevertheless impacted on education. Some changes have been specific to Wales, and details will be provided later in this chapter. Significantly, few of the new policies have been framed or developed with gender equality in mind and, indeed, there is little explicit reference to gender equality in policy documentation. There have also been various changes in understanding and definition of equal opportunities, in the gendered patterns of pupil performance and in the extent of involvement in equal opportunities by schools and LEAs. All these factors provide the context for the current study.

The main aim of this chapter is to provide an understanding of previous polices and patterns against which the findings of the project can be judged and compared. The first section reviews earlier equal opportunities strategies and policy-making, identifying the principal concerns of teachers and researchers prior to the late 1980s. In particular, it focuses on whether changing patterns and trends might be perceived as a continuation of earlier educational or cultural shifts in society towards gender equality. The second section focuses on the reforms themselves, outlining the main characteristics of each and providing short descriptions of policy intentions and any subsequent developments. The third section suggests a dual form of categorisation for the educational reforms which is used as a basis for the research analysis, and the final sections consider in what ways the discourse of equal opportunities has been influenced by the introduction of ideologies of choice and the market into the policy and practice of education.

2.1   OVERVIEW OF RESEARCH ON GENDER PRIOR TO THE REFORMS

Equality has been a target of government policy-making at various stages in the twentieth century. From the 1944 Education Act onwards, 'equality of opportunity' was included in the rhetoric of schooling, whether in the 1940s focused on education appropriate to perceived levels of intelligence, or in the 1960s concerned with eradicating social class differences, or on increased gender and racial equality from the 1970s onwards. Indeed, the 1960s and 1970s were strongly influenced by concerns about equality of opportunity, both in the political arena and in social and educational research.

9

In fact, before 1979, policies under both Labour and Conservative governments were orientated towards the twin goals of greater equality and increased economic growth - with the former seen as contributing to the latter. The main legislation associated with equal opportunities at this time were the Equal Pay Act (1970, coming into force in 1975) the Sex Discrimination Act (1975) with specifically included education, and with respect to 'race' issues, the Race Relations Act (1976), a new Act replacing previous legislation. This set of legislation led to a range of policy strategies instituted by individual teachers, schools and local authorities, many of whom were anxious to see enacted the spirit as well as the letter of the legislation. The most positive impact of the SDA included improving equality of access to all subjects of the curriculum and the role of the EOC in ensuring that legal requirements were understood and complied with.

However, by 1979, partly as a consequence of Prime Minister James Callaghan's speech (1976) at Ruskin College which signalled the end of the post-war boom period and an increasing concern for value-for-money in education, a debate had begun to develop about the extent to which policies aimed at increased equality might be at odds with those aimed at economic growth and individual accountability (David 1980).

At the same time, a number of consistent research findings began to emerge pointing to inadequacies in schooling for girls and young women. For example, studies showed that teachers had lower expectations of girls than boys (as did parents and the pupils themselves), were more intellectually encouraging to, and demanding of boys, yet rewarded girls for good behaviour and appropriately feminine behaviour (Maccoby and Jacklin 1974). They also allowed boys to be naughtier than girls in the classroom and playground, and gave boys more attention (Clarricoates 1978). Moreover, due to racism as well as sexism, black pupils of both sexes were found to attract more, and largely negative teacher attention than their white counterparts (Wright 1987).

In terms of the formal curriculum, syllabuses and content were found to exclude the experiences of girls and women (whether white or black). At secondary level, where choice was available, girls tended to opt for humanities, languages and social science, and boys for science, mathematics and technological subjects (Pratt et al. 1984). Also, students were frequently directed into traditionally male and female subjects and careers, and in the main, girls' careers were believed to be less important than those of boys' (Arnot and Weiner 1987).

In terms of performance, girls were generally found to be achieving well at primary level although they tended to slip back at secondary level, particularly in Mathematics and Science (Kelly 1985; Burton 1986). Boys' poor performance in English and Modern Languages in primary and secondary school was seen to be offset by their increasingly better performance in examinations as they reached school-leaving age (Spender 1980). In general, young men were seen to have an advantage in the labour market because many young women had low occupational aspirations, tending to opt for low status and low paid 'feminine' jobs to bridge the gap between leaving school and marriage.

The hidden or unwritten curriculum of schooling was also found to exert pressure on students (and staff) to conform in gender-specific ways; for example, there were different rules on uniform and discipline for girls and boys, and sexual harassment and verbal abuse were found to be common features of school life (Lees 1987).

As a consequence, by the early 1980s, some teachers and advisory staff (and Her Majesty's Inspectors of Schools (HMI) - see Orr 1984) began to develop a range of strategies in order to counter these inequalities. These included: persuading secondary students to opt for non-traditional subjects such as Physics for girls and Modern Languages for boys; encouraging wider career aspiration through non-discriminatory careers' advice; revising reading schemes and school texts to make them less sexist and more inclusive; 'de-sexing' registers and 'uni-sexing' school uniform; appointing female senior staff as positive role models for female pupils; establishing equal opportunities working parties, policy statements and posts of responsibility and so on (Weiner and Arnot 1987).

The main concerns at this time were: at primary level, helping girls to become more assertive and removing sexist practices from the formal and hidden curriculum; and at secondary schools, raising the profile of young women in the labour market, persuading girls into Science and Mathematics (there was little focus on boys at this time), and the perceived decline of girls' performance and self-confidence during adolescence (Whyte 1983; Millman 1987; Chisholm and Holland 1986; Whyld 1983).

Towards the mid-1980s, however, the scenario began to change as LEAs with a commitment to increasing equal opportunity began to put pressure on teachers to move towards linking a range of equal opportunities themes. Policies were formulated which addressed gender, race and

11

ethnicity, class and disability with emphasis moving towards integrating work on gender into overall school policy, organisation and disciplinary structures and across the curriculum (see ILEA 1986a, b).

The period from the mid-1970s until the mid-1980s, thus, might be viewed as one where the extent of equal opportunities development, although underpinned by legislation, depended on the commitment of individual politicians, teachers and local authorities. Equal opportunities policy development, hence, might originate from local political allegiance, individual teachers or headteachers, an 'awareness raising' incident or involvement in one of several funded curriculum development projects (Whyte et al. 1984; Millman and Weiner 1985). Initiatives were often short-term, small-scale, temporary and local, and the national picture was difficult to ascertain. Also, there was little opportunity to evaluate the long-term effects of any policies and practices, though short-term evaluations suggested that the perceptions of some teachers (and pupils) were changing (Whyte et al. 1984; ILEA 1986a, b).

By the late 1980s, as the government's increasing emphasis on achievement and standards took hold, research on gender began to shift away from emphasis on policy and practice towards investigation of patterns of difference in examinations, and between girls and boys of different social groups (Gipps and Murphy 1994). This coincided with the beginning of the educational reforms and thus researchers' analyses also switched to ascertaining the significance and likely effects of the Educational Reform Act and of the National Curriculum (see, for example, Arnot 1989; Burton and Weiner 1990; Miles and Middleton 1990; Shah 1990; David 1993).

Evidence that girls' patterns of achievement were changing began to emerge in a range of subject-focused studies in the early 1980s (reported in Gipps and Murphy 1994). Most notable of these were the research of the Assessment of Performance Unit (APU) and international surveys of achievement in English, Mathematics and Science. More recent studies identified a range of possible reasons for this improvement; for example, changes in assessment modes in relation to tasks and skills, and the amount of designated coursework in examinations. More recently, Schools Examination and Assessment Council (SEAC) commissioned research on GCSE performance in English and Mathematics (Stobart et al. 1992) suggested that gender differences in these subjects have been affected by factors such as differentiated entry schemes and school setting practices, the selection of topics, teacher expectations, pupil anxiety and motivation and familiarity with the context of tasks and modes of assessing.

12

Also of concern has been the so-called underachievement of boys' relative to girls' achievement patterns. Attention has been drawn to boys' lower performance in reading and in other literary skills, especially in primary school, and their later performance in English and Modern Foreign Languages (OFSTED 1993a). Such male underachievement has been used to imply that girls may no longer face previously identified difficulties in school; and indeed, some would suggest that it is boys who are now at a disadvantage.

2.2 THE REFORM ERA: SPECIFIC REFORMS

The educational reforms within the time frame of 1984-1994 with which the project has been particularly concerned are, in chronological order:

- The New Training Initiative (1981) which led to a proliferation of pre-vocational courses, including the Certificate of Pre-Vocational Education (CPVE), Business and Technological Education Council (BTEC) and others attempting to place value on and rationalise vocational education provision for 14-18 year olds.

- The Technical, Educational and Vocational Initiative (TVEI) (1983) which was initially a pilot experiment in 14 LEAs aimed at stimulating curriculum development in technical and vocational subjects for the 14-18 age range in schools and colleges. Through various extension phases in its decade or more of existence, TVEI has had a major impact on secondary schools nationally. Of particular interest to the project has been the requirement that efforts should be made within TVEI to overcome sex-stereotyping.

- Changes in examinations for 16 year olds at the end of secondary school, particularly the introduction of GCSE (1985 for implementation in 1988), which combined General Certificate of Education (GCE) O-level examinations with the more recently introduced Certificate for Secondary Education (CSE). These changes provided new criteria for examination and assessment which included increased use of coursework.

- Creation of the National Council for Vocational Qualifications from the *Training for Jobs* (1984) legislation which led to the development of National Vocational Qualifications (NVQs) and General National Vocational Qualifications (GNVQs) introduced in 1986. The principal aim was to ensure that the needs of industry were

13

served by the provision of new courses and qualifications based on the acquisition of work skills and competencies, principally for 16 plus students in colleges (later introduced in schools).

- The Education Act (1986), and particularly:
  - The creation of new governing bodies for every school with representative parent governors.
  - The provision for sex education and associated social and health education.

- The Education Reform Act (ERA) (1988) and particularly:
  - Implementation of the National Curriculum (Core subjects: English, Mathematics and Science, and Welsh[1] in Welsh Medium schools; Foundation subjects: Art, History, Geography, Modern Foreign Language (MFL), Music, Technology and Physical Education).
  - Creation of the National Curriculum Council (NCC) to oversee curricular developments.
  - Introduction of Standardized Assessment Targets (SATs) Key Stages 1-4 within the National Curriculum.
  - Creation of the Schools Examination and Assessment Council to oversee examination and assessment.
  - Implementation of local management of schools (LMS) giving stronger powers to governing bodies and devolving school budgets.
  - Open enrolment for schools, requiring schools to accept pupils up to capacity.
  - Provisions for opting out of schools from the LEA and the associated creation of Grant Maintained Schools (GMS) and the associated Grant Maintained Schools Trust.
  - Development of City Technology Colleges (CTCs), funded jointly by the public and private sectors, to promote a stronger commercial, technical and practical element into urban schooling.

---

[1] In Wales, Welsh is taught as an additional core subject where the medium of instruction in schools is Welsh. In all other Welsh schools it is an additional Foundation subject to those specified in the National Curriculum.

- Introduction of the *Citizen's Charter* (1991) giving users of public services greater rights and standards of performance; and especially the Parent's Charter *You and Your Child's Education*.

- The Education (Schools) Act (1992) and particularly:
  - Abolition of HMI and the creation of the Office for Standards in Education as a relatively autonomous body.
  - Introduction of a new system of regular, statutory inspections for schools, conducted by members of OFSTED.
  - Increased requirements for the sex education curriculum and the role of parents.

- Publication of the White Paper: *Choice and Diversity: A New Framework for Schools* (1992) which set the framework for the 1993 legislation and argued for more parental choice and diversity of educational provision;

- The Education Act (1993) and particularly:
  - Encouragement to increase the number of grant maintained schools.
  - The reduced role of LEAs.
  - Introduction of statutory requirements for performance tables of school examinations, particularly at the end of compulsory schooling (16 plus) and for A-levels.
  - Creation of the Funding Agency for Schools (FAS) which assumes some of the responsibilities of LEAs for grant maintained schools.

- The Dearing Report (SCAA 1993) which led to:
  - A more streamlined National Curriculum with the introduction of curriculum choice at KS3.
  - Greater administrative efficiency through combining NCC and SEAC into the Schools Assessment Authority (SCAA).

2.3   THE WELSH REFORM CONTEXT

Wales, unlike Scotland, has tended to be assimilated into the English education system and has been subject to the same reforms, though with variations that take into account local structures and organisation. For example, the Office of Her Majesty's Chief Inspector (OHMCI) is the Welsh equivalent of England's OFSTED; the Curriculum Council for Wales (CCW), established in 1988, was the Welsh equivalent of SEAC; and the Curriculum and Assessment Authority for Wales (ACAC), established in 1994, is currently the Welsh equivalent of SCAA.

Significantly, the 1988 ERA changed the status of the Welsh language by making it a compulsory subject for *all* pupils in Wales up to KS4 (though the Dearing Report subsequently moderated some of the compulsory requirements from KS3 onwards). However, the addition of Welsh as both a core (in Welsh Medium schools) and Foundation subject (in other Welsh schools) in the National Curriculum has meant that Welsh pupils take more National Curriculum subjects than their English counterparts with little apparent recognition for the extra work incurred. Other National Curriculum subjects generally remain the same for England and Wales, though Wales currently has different curricula for Music, Art, History, Geography, Religious Education and Welsh for first and second language pupils.

There have also been differences in the impact on Wales of other education reforms; for example, fewer Welsh than English schools have opted out (in 1992, 15 out of 1,947 Welsh schools were GMS); and there are no Welsh CTCs, nor have any been proposed.

It is also important to note that, during the period of the project, plans were being made to replace the eight existing Welsh LEAs with 21 'multi-purpose' authorities having wider responsibility than for education alone.

2.4 CATEGORISING THE REFORMS: CENTRAL CONTROL OR DIVERSITY

The educational reforms as depicted above may be viewed variously as seeking to bring about change in educational standards, economic policy and/or political control of schooling. Not surprisingly therefore, they have drawn much comment although proving difficult to characterise since they are neither homogeneous nor aimed at one particular policy objective or outcome.

To aid the analysis of findings, the project drew on Whitty's (1989) perception of the reforms as having two contradictory policy thrusts: the first aiming to assert greater central control over schools, through for example, the creation of a National Curriculum and regular inspections and the second encouraging choice, competition and marketisation of schools through the introduction of self-managing schools and new types of school provision. The framework of analysis adopted for the project thus distinguishes between curricular and organisational reforms as follows:

Curricular reforms - Developments and changes in the school curriculum and in vocational education; assessment and related forms of testing and examination; monitoring of school performance; tables of school examinations and results.

Organisational reforms - Developments and changes in the organisation and control of schools; shifts from LEA provision to greater diversity of school type with open enrolment, GMS and CTCs; increased power of school governing bodies.

It might be argued that changes in the school curriculum and associated testing and monitoring of performance explicitly concerned with improving educational standards for *all* pupils are more 'equality-friendly' than organisational changes aimed at greater individual choice and diversity of schooling. The Education Reform Act might also be seen as a pivotal piece of legislation designed to create a 'new era' in education in which both tendencies operate in tandem in a combined effort to improve professional practices of previous eras. One aim of the research was therefore to investigate which policy trend might be seen as more conducive to equal opportunities.

2.5   REINTERPRETING EQUALITY

As already noted, few of the educational reforms directly focused on equality issues and, in fact, there is no one agreed definition of what is meant or understood by equal opportunities. Previous interpretations relating to gender tended to focus on equalising experiences and achievements of girls and boys. However, as we have seen, at various times equal opportunities has been used to address different forms of educational or socio-economic inequality (including 'race', gender, class, disability, religion, ethnicity, sexual orientation, age). Moreover there have been distinct differences in how equal opportunities is conceptualised; for example, liberal and other, more radical conceptions of equal opportunities differ in specifying what kinds of action are needed (see Weiner 1994, for a more detailed discussion of perspectives and approaches). Riley (1994) suggests that recent strategies for change have been premised on one of two interpretations: 'equality of opportunity' and 'equality of outcome'.

The liberal interpretation of equality, equality of opportunity, has been concerned with ensuring that the rules of the game (employment, or access to courses, or examinations) are set out fairly. The assumption has been that rigorous administrative controls and formalized systems will ensure that fair play takes place...

The more radical conception of equality, equality of outcome, has been concerned with widening access... through action designed to redress past imbalances. It has been an essentially interventionist strategy aimed at redistributing resources and opportunities to disadvantaged groups.
(Riley 1994, p. 13)

Thus, it could be argued that raising standards can be equated with liberal (rather than radical) concepts of equality of opportunity in the sense of aiming to improve performance *for all students*. Indeed, some of the education policies have clearly tried to accomplish this, the clearest example being key stage testing of the National Curriculum. Changes in secondary school examinations, such as GCSE, and TVEI in its pilot and extension phases, could also be said to focus on an improved curriculum access for all students. Equally, the development and rationalisation of vocational qualifications may also have been expected to have a similar impact.

The creation of OFSTED and the legislative requirements in the form of regular (four-year) inspection visits have also changed forms of monitoring of performance, and indeed it could be argued, extended public accountability to standards in education. In so doing, OFSTED has required information on equal opportunities prior to inspection visits, on for example, the existence of school policy, curriculum access, student enrolment and staffing (OFSTED 1993b). (See Chapters 5 and 6 for further discussion of OFSTED's role here). The aim of this was, presumably, to highlight the importance of equality issues for *all* schools.

In contrast, other policy initiatives have focused on increased choice and diversity of provision from which individuals might choose that which is most suited to their needs and wishes. Open enrolment has ostensibly enabled parents to choose from a wider range of schools for their children and parents have an increased presence on school governing bodies. Another example is the *Citizen's Charter* which was introduced as an expression of commitment to ensuring standards of public service fitted to the needs of the individual. The Charter was expanded to include education where significantly, parents (rather than LEAs or teachers) were seen as the main arbiters of educational standards for children. Publication of *The Parent's Charter: You and Your Child's Education* thus gave explicit recognition to individual parents' pivotal role in education (David 1993). The point at issue here is to what extent the rights of individual (usually middle-class) parents to promote their children's interests at the expense of others can be seen as running counter to equal opportunities considerations.

2.6   REFORM IMPLEMENTATION

In reviewing the impact of the reforms upon gender trends and patterns in schools, it should be noted that at the time of the project many of the policy changes had only just begun to take effect in schools. In particular, curricular reforms were introduced gradually and in transitional forms and the linking of GCSE to the National Curriculum proved more complicated than anticipated. Moreover, some parts of the Education Reform Act, for example, concerning assessment, proved too complex to implement fully, resulting in various forms of avoidance, amendment or teacher action. In the event, a series of reviews of the reforms resulted in the Dearing Report in 1993 and the subsequent down-scaling of the requirements of the National Curriculum and associated assessment procedures.

Additionally, public and/or independent schools were not compelled to teach the National Curriculum, though many chose to do so. Ironically, the introduction of the first set of 'private' league tables and second set of performance tables for the entire range of state and independent schools have had the effect, in reality, of producing similar academic targets for all secondary schools.

The creation of a market or 'quasi-markets' in which practices from the private sector have been introduced into public services focusing on the individual consumer or customer, and the introduction of the community charge and later, the council tax, have brought about yet more changes in the relationships of schooling and between central and local government. Simultaneously, new kinds of economic accountability were produced through the developments of LMS, GMS, CTCs and, more recently, with the Funding Agency for Schools which has replaced LEAs in areas where the majority of schools have opted out of local authority control. A number of semi-autonomous agencies in education have also been created with diverse functional roles; these include SCAA, OFSTED and the Teachers Training Agency (TTA) and the involvement of lay people as school governors and OFSTED inspectors.

2.7   CONCLUSIONS

- Equal opportunities has been a target for education policy makers since 1944, though at various times different aspects of equality have been emphasised more than others. Only after the passage of the Sex Discrimination in 1975 did gender equality become an issue for educationists, and then for only the 'committed'.

- In the decade 1975-1985, a wide number of concerns emerged pointing to girls' disadvantage in the schooling process, and a number of strategies were developed to counter the various inequalities. However, policy-making was dependent on committed individuals or initiatives and thus tended to be short-term and small-scale.

- Following 1985, the educational reforms marked a change in direction for schools and LEAs. In terms of their implications for gender equality, the reforms can be divided into two sets: those concerned with curriculum, assessment and achievement and those concerned with the organisations of schools.

- An aim of the research has been to identify which of the sets of reforms have been most 'equality friendly' and in what ways.

3 THE GENDER GAP IN SUBJECT CHOICE AND EXAMINATION PERFORMANCE UP TO AND INCLUDING GCSE

This chapter describes the current profile of gender differences in compulsory education and, in particular the gender gaps in subject choice and performance at 16+ over the ten-year period. Such patterns have been affected by a range of curriculum and assessment policies and reforms including the introduction of GCSE examinations and the National Curriculum (as we have seen in Chapter 2).

It first discusses gender patterns in national assessment, at primary levels and in examination entry and performance at GCSE (including GCE O-levels and CSE) for four age cohorts. The final section compares recent patterns of performance at GCSE in mixed- and single-sex schools.

The data presented consider the performance of male and female students as a changing proportion of their entry patterns over the ten year period. The concern is not whether more girls or boys achieved high grades in a subject but whether equal proportions of male and female students who entered examinations at 16 achieved high grades (defined here as A-C grades for the GCSE). The concept of a *gender gap* makes it possible to trace over time any differences between male and female pupils in entry and performance in specific curriculum subjects.

3.1 GENDER AND NATIONAL ASSESSMENT

As much of the available data on national assessment remain based, at the time of writing, upon pilot schools and pilot evaluation studies, it is not possible to offer a comprehensive analysis of the consequences of the reforms for male and female educational attainment in each National Curriculum subject. The SATs data are of interest, however, in so far as they highlight emerging trends and gender concerns.

Key Stage 1 (Age 7)

Early indications from pilot schemes for SATs suggest that girls perform better than boys at all ages, whatever the test. For example, in 1992, when some 600,000 children (aged seven) were assessed formally in English, Mathematics, Science and Technology, the differences between boys' and girls' performance were marked. The results from England and Wales (which included over 2,000 children from independent schools) demonstrated that a higher proportion of female than male pupils achieved Level 1 and Level 2, especially in English where the proportion who attained at least Level 2 was for girls 11 percentage points higher than for boys (CSO 1994, p. 50). Perhaps more unexpected was the relatively high achievement of girls in Science and Technology.

The extent to which gender differences are already present in attainment levels on entering school is perhaps less appreciated. In 1994, 3,278 children in reception Year R (4-5 years old) were screened on a range of nine different skills and the following patterns were found (shown in Figure 3.1).

Figure 3.1   Performance of girls and boys on the Year R screening

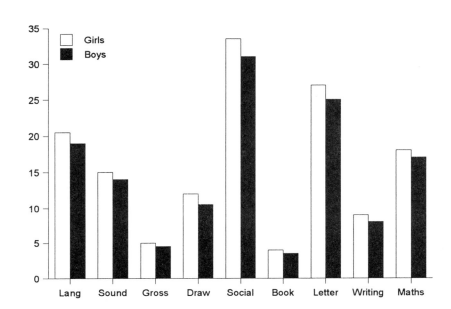

Source: Surrey County Council, 1994

The report also claimed that:

> *Girls significantly outperformed boys on all assessments except the gross motor skills assessment. All these differences except early age gross motor skills are statistically significant (p < 0.001). This indicates that girls at this age in Surrey schools appear to have an advantage over boys. This difference in performance is reflected in the Year 3 reading results.... where girls outperform boys in*

reading ability. ...The differences in the screening assessments are greatest in the areas of social skills, letter identification, writing and drawing a girl or boy. (Surrey County Council 1994, p.4)

The explanation offered by the authors of the report suggests that the ways in which 'boys and girls are socialised, or managed by parents and carers' might prepare girls better for entry to schooling. In the study, pupils who attended pre-school provision had higher attainment levels - pre-school attendance perhaps might therefore be particularly valuable for improving the lower attainment of boys and of bilingual pupils. The report concludes that 'serious consideration needs to be given to boys' under-performance in relation to girls' (Surrey County Council 1994).

Other data on gender performance are available through the evaluation of pilot studies for Key Stage 1 (SCAA 1994a). A number of studies have considered the relationship between teacher assessment and formal tests, and the ways in which gender issues might affect overall results. In summarising this evidence Gipps and Murphy (1994) suggest the following:

That significant gender differences can be found in the distribution of boys and girls across the different levels of attainment and between subjects. On the whole girls appear to be achieving higher grades in all subjects, but particularly in English and scoring in the middle range in Mathematics and Science.

Teacher assessment may be an important factor in examination success, since they are implicated in the placing of boys at extreme ends of the grading scheme (Levels 1 and 3) and the clustering of girls at Level 2, especially in Mathematics. In Science, girls' work in Biology and boys' work in Physics are likely to be rated as particularly good.

Key Stages 2 and 3 (Age 11 and 14)

Girls are also succeeding at Key Stage 2 although the information available thus far, 'should not be used to make judgements about national standards' (SCAA 1994b, p. 9). In 1994, 85 per cent of English teachers, 84 per cent of Mathematics teachers and 70 per cent of Science teachers reported that the levels of achieved by their children in the pilot (shown in the Figures 3.3, 3.4 and 3.5) 'matched their expectations'. The results were as follows:

23

Figure 3.2   **Levels achieved in English, 1994 pilot KS2**

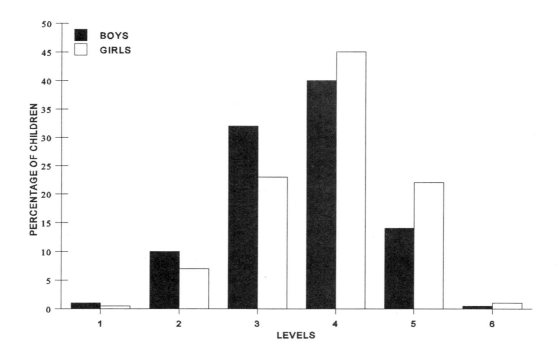

Figure 3.3   **Levels achieved in Mathematics, 1994 pilot KS2**

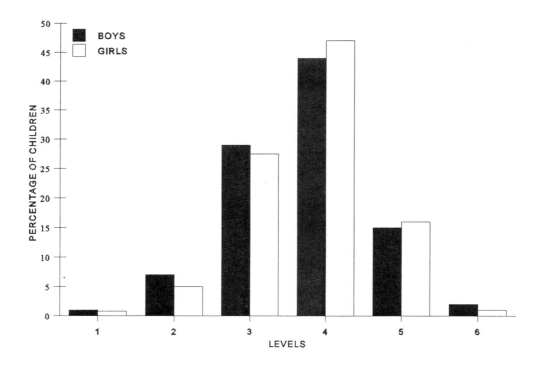

Figure 3.4   Levels achieved in Science, 1994 pilot KS2

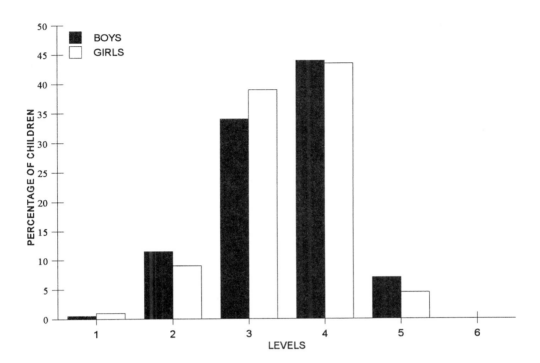

Studies of Key Stage 3 assessments from a range of consortia also suggest that overall girls are achieving higher levels of attainment than boys (SCAA 1994c,d,e). What has additionally been signalled in such studies, however, is the importance of considering male and female patterns amongst pupils from different ethnic groups and bilingual communities.

The evaluations of the pilot SATs have been particularly important in confirming the need to contextualise the gender performance gap. Gipps and Murphy (1994) summarise the range of factors that might be involved in accounting for differential performance on SATs:

> *A general picture emerges at ages seven (in 1990 and 1991) and 14 (in 1991)*
> *of girls scoring higher than boys particularly in English and Maths; more boys*
> *scoring at the extremes; minority ethnic groups scoring lower than 'white'*
> *children; those whose home language is not English scoring significantly less*
> *well; teacher assessments are lower than the SAT score for children from ethnic*
> *minorities and/or whose home language is not English.*
> (p.205)

25

Summary

Especially in the early years of schooling, SATs reveal distinct gender differences in achievement scores in particular components and subjects. Some boys excel, especially in Science and Mathematics; yet others perform poorly compared with girls (particularly in English). Though girls excel in English, otherwise their performance levels tend to cluster around the mean. In contrast, boys perform at the extremes.

Such gender differences at primary level need to be considered in the light of a range of social and educational factors. Previous research on gender differences in very young children suggests that girls start with an early advantage in a broad range of skills. There is no current evidence to show that such patterns have been altered by the National Curriculum. Pilot studies of SATs also suggest that success in assessment is affected by the gender of pupils as well as other factors, such as ethnic origin, home language and special needs.

3.2 THE GENDER GAP IN GCSE ENTRIES AND PERFORMANCE

As already noted, a number of key reforms in curriculum and assessment were introduced within the ten-year period covered by this study. What is being assessed has changed as much as the modes of assessment. New subject clusters have been created and new courses developed, the most significant being the introduction in 1988 of the GCSE, (replacing the GCE O-level and CSE) and the National Curriculum.

In 1985, a two-tier system of examining at 16 existed; GCE O-level, taken by the top achievers and CSE, generally seen as targeting the average student, grade 1 of which was considered the equivalent of an O-level pass. In 1988 these two examinations were integrated to form the GCSE examination, with the eventual aim that most children in Year 11 would take at least five subjects.

Since 1985 there has been an increase in Year 11 pupils entering public examinations (from 91 per cent to 96 per cent). However, changes in the cohort sizes of the entries for English reveal that the numbers of male students have decreased from nearly half a million in 1985 to just over 304,000 in 1994. The number of female students has dropped proportionally even further, from outnumbering males by over 30,000 in 1985 to 2,000 fewer female students than male students in 1994.

In almost every subject area the greatest increase in entry, relative to cohort size for both boys and girls, occurred between 1985 (a year before GCSE was first introduced) and 1988 (when the first GCSE examinations took place).

Defining the gender gap at GCSE

In order to identify the changing gender gap in examinations at 16+ over the ten-year period (1985-1995) it was decided to examine separately examination entry patterns and the attainment of qualifications, as identified by high level of performance at GCSE (identified as A-C grades).

An index was calculated to assess the changing proportions of male and female students in each of the four selected 'snapshot' years - 1985, 1988, 1991 and 1994 - on the basis of who entered and who achieved high grades in selected subjects. (The index, and its rationale, are described more fully in Appendix A). The basis for the calculations is an estimation of the age cohort (the number of students in Year 11 taking GCSE) calculated separately for male and female students which is used to index both entry and performance. The patterns therefore reflect trends that are not conflated with changes in the absolute size of male or female cohorts.

The ratio of male entry to female entry makes it possible to identify those subjects which were more likely to be chosen by male or female students. In the histogram describing each subject, the *entry gender gap* is shown by plotting the proportions of the age cohort who took the examination in the subject in each year.

The proportions of entry (for each of the selected years) of male and female students who had achieved A-C grades for a selected range of GCSE subjects is also used to assess the *gender performance gap* in the different subject areas over time.

By comparing the gender gap in performance with the gender gap in entry it is possible to identify which sex is achieving particularly well or badly. Thus, if the size of the performance gender gap is greater than the entry gender gap, then the sex which is predominant in relation to entry is achieving better than could be normally anticipated; if it is narrower, then the predominant sex in terms of entry is performing at a lower level than would normally be anticipated. A graph for each subject is provided which shows whether the performance gap is in favour of girls (+) or whether it is in favour of boys (-). Equality in terms of performance between the sexes would be indicated if the line approaches zero.

English, Mathematics and Science

First, the three core National Curriculum subjects - English, Science and Mathematics - are considered. For English (which evolved from English Language as it was formerly known, but which also contains a literature element) the entry gender gap is, by definition, zero - but this is not the case for performance. In 1985, single and double award Science did not exist in their current form, showing initially in the 1991 'snapshot' year for this study. The Science Double Award currently dominates the Science GCSE entry, at the expense of the three separate Sciences. Figure 3.5 shows the increasing take-up of Science by both sexes and the closing entry gender gap for the cluster of Science subjects for the four snapshot years.

Figure 3.5   **GCSE Science entry**

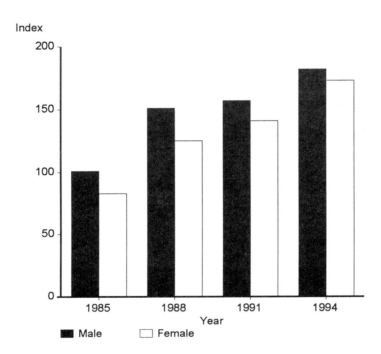

The entry gender gap for Science subjects has decreased and shows a marked change since 1985 (a drop from 9.5 per cent to 2.5 per cent); but it is not clear whether the gap started reducing substantially between 1985 and 1988 with the onset of GCSE. It is also not obvious whether the decrease in the entry gender gap is the result of girls taking fewer Science options, or, latterly, more girls opting for the single award rather than the double award, the latter of which counts as two subjects in the index calculations.

Figure 3.6   **GCSE Mathematics entry**

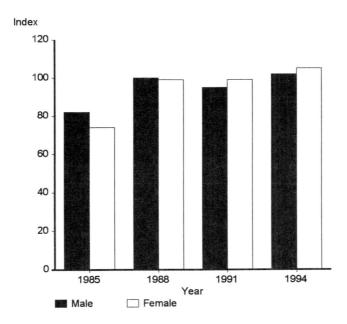

GCSE Mathematics is a subject which includes entries in Statistics and Additional Mathematics. By 1994, the whole age cohort appeared to take some form of Mathematics, with the gender entry gap substantially reduced, and indeed marginally *reversed* in favour of female students (5.5 per cent in 1985 to 1.5 per cent in 1994).

For English GCSE, the high performance gender gap in favour of female students has continued, compared with the marked reduction of gender gap in the other two core National Curriculum subjects. However, English is the only subject of the three in which female students have predominated since 1985. Figure 3.7 below illustrates the change in gender gap with positive values indicating females performing better than expectation and negative values indicating males performing better than expectation.

There has been a notable move towards gender equality in Science and Mathematics at GCSE, which, in 1985, showed a clear gender gap in performance in favour of male students. Changes to examining procedures in Science may partly be the reason, although the separate sciences of Physics, Chemistry and Biology, though much depleted in entry, also exhibit similar declines in expected male performance.

In English, where females have traditionally done well, the gender gap in performance has not only continued but there was also an improvement in female performance in 1988 when the first

GCSE examinations took place. Female students have continued to perform better than expected, despite the fact that, with the introduction of the National Curriculum, English has been (from 1994 onwards) examined partly by examination rather than by the original hundred per cent coursework regime thought to favour girls.

Figure 3.7   The gender gap in relative performance for core National Curriculum subjects

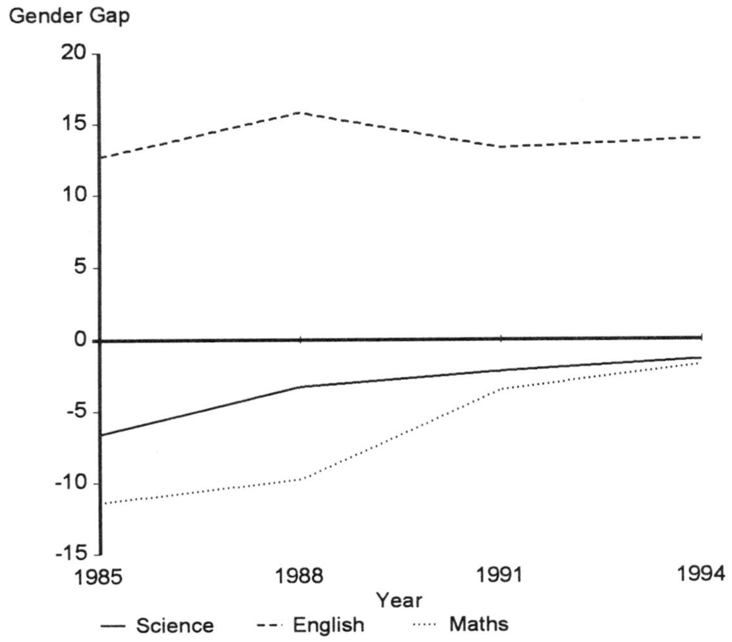

Technology

Technology is one of the foundation subjects of the National Curriculum and, according to Moon (1994), is a major innovation for the National Curriculum, since it was not in existence as a subject previously. It is compulsory up to KS3 (Year 9) and optional thereafter. It combines Craft, Design and Technology (CDT), with a conventionally higher male entry, and Home Economics, with a conventionally higher female entry.

It might be anticipated that the inclusion of Technology in the National Curriculum would have led to an increase in those taking the subject. However, from a peak in 1988 there has been a fairly steady decline in take-up of Technology by both boys and girls and reasons for the decline do not appear to be gender-related, 19 per cent in 1985 down to 12 per cent in 1994. Although the gender entry gap has closed since 1985, it is still considerably in favour of boys. Nevertheless, those girls who enter gain better than expected results, a trend that has become more pronounced since 1985. The performance gender gap is given in Figure 3.9, illustrating how girls have increasingly performed better than boys in Technology.

Figure 3.8   **GCSE Technology entry**

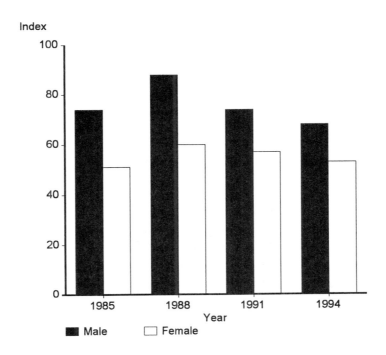

Figure 3.9   **The gender gap in relative performance for Technology**

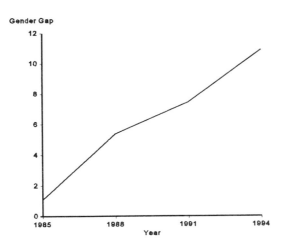

English Literature and Modern Foreign Languages

English Literature and Modern Foreign Languages are considered together as they share similar gender patterns for entry and performance. English is a National Curriculum core subject and as a defined criterion for this study has an entry of 100 for both males and females for each year of the study. In contrast, English Literature is optional with a pattern of entries as illustrated in Figure 3.10.

Figure 3.10   GCSE English Literature entry

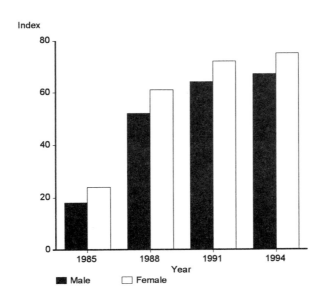

Both male and female entry increased considerably over the period and there appears to have been little change in the gender gap with a larger female take-up being maintained. However, as a proportion of the total entry, the gap has more than halved over the ten years (a drop from 13 per cent in 1984 to 6 per cent in 1994).

Drama, though a minority subject, has also seen an increase in take-up throughout the period, with the percentage of males entering the subject consistently about half that for females.

The cluster of Modern Foreign Languages, of which the largest is French, shows a similar pattern to other subjects with higher female entry. Although there has been a steady rise in the proportion of male and female students, there appears to be a similar pattern of gender gap entries to those found for English Literature, i.e. the gender gap has reduced from 20 per cent in 1984 to 9 per cent in 1994. This is shown in Figure 3.11.

Both English and Modern Foreign Languages have entries with higher proportions of female students, though the entry gender gap is decreasing. Performance relative to entry for the two subjects is shown in Figure 3.12. English Literature shows girls predominating in entry figures and achieving strong performances (especially in 1988).

The inclusion of Modern Foreign Languages in the National Curriculum appears to have contributed to the substantial increase in take-up of the subject by both male and female students. Notwithstanding this rise in entry, the high female performance in Modern Foreign Languages has increased for each snapshot year.

Figure 3.11   **GCSE Modern Foreign Language entry**

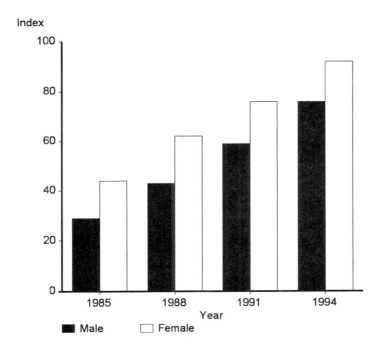

The Humanities: Geography and History

Geography and History show slightly different patterns over the ten-year period and, post-Dearing are no longer compulsory at KS4. As Figure 3.13 shows, the entry gender gap in Geography peaked in 1988 at 19 per cent, but has been decreasing slowly since then to 14 per cent in 1994. Numbers taking History have tended to be lower, with male and female entries almost identical since the first GCSE examination year of 1988.

33

Figure 3.12   **The gender gap in relative performance for English Literature and Modern Foreign Languages**

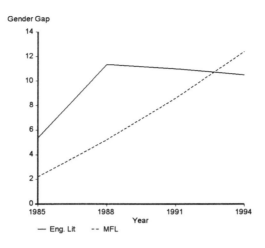

The Humanities: Geography and History

Geography and History show slightly different patterns over the ten-year period and, post-Dearing are no longer compulsory at KS4.   As Figure 3.13 shows, the entry gender gap in Geography peaked in 1988 at 19 per cent, but has been decreasing slowly since then to 14 per cent in 1994.   Numbers taking History have tended to be lower, with male and female entries almost identical since the first GCSE examination year of 1988.

Figure 3.13   **GCSE Geography and History entries**

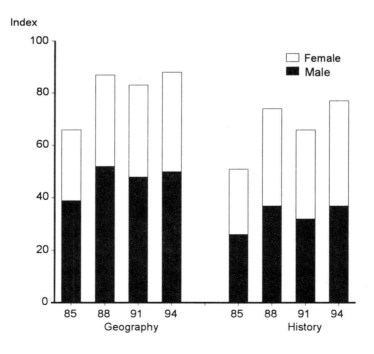

Despite the entry gender gap in favour of girls for Geography, and the gender gap in favour of male students in History, the pattern for both in performance shows that girls gain more A-C grades than expected and boys fewer. Again there is a clear peak in 1988, and, as Figure 3.14 shows, female achievement in A-C grades is increasing.

Figure 3.14   The gender gap in relative performance for History and Geography

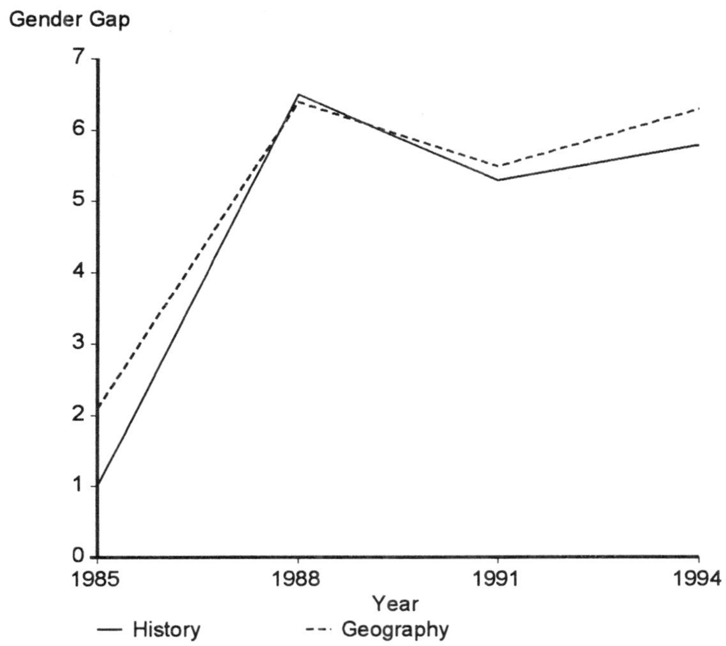

The Arts

The Art and Design subject cluster (which includes Art, History of Art and Art and Design) has seen an increase in entry for both sexes from 1985 to 1994 with the consequences that the comparative gender equity in entry in 1985 has more recently shifted to a slightly higher female entry.

It can also be seen from Figure 3.16 that there is a gender performance gap in favour of higher female performance, which is, however, decreasing slightly.

Figure 3.15   **GCSE Art and Design entry**

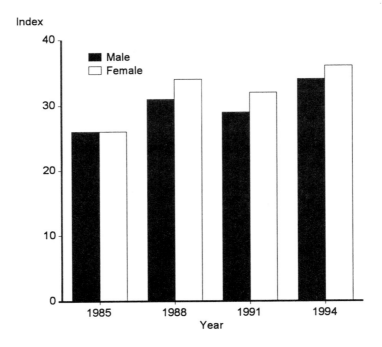

Figure 3.16   **The gender gap in relative performance for Art and Design**

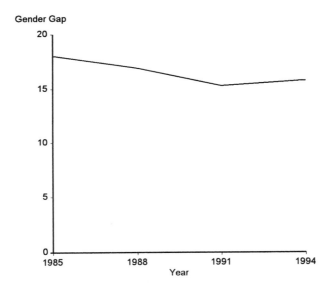

Social Sciences

Social Sciences is the only cluster of subjects whose entry dropped between 1985 and 1988. Economics and Social Studies are the two largest subjects in this cluster (which includes Sociology), and of these two only the Social Studies entry appears to have regained its 1985 position.   The entry gender gap in favour of female students rose from 19 per cent in 1984 to 42 per cent in 1994.

The Vocational Studies cluster has attracted an entry gender gap in favour of female students (33 per cent in 1994) with both boys and girls exhibiting maximum levels of entry in 1988, which then declined fairly sharply to 1994.   This cluster of subjects has probably been more affected than most by the introduction of compulsory curricula and the reduction of choice.   The three subject areas of Economics, Social and Vocational Studies, though small in entry numbers, illustrate an unpredictability which demonstrates the dangers of generalisation.   In Economics boys performed better than girls in 1985 but the performance gap since then has been substantially reduced, to almost nil in 1994.   Social Studies and Vocational Studies exhibit different patterns of relative performance, with the gender gap in favour of girls decreasing slightly in Social Studies and the gender gap in favour of girls increasing slightly for Vocational Studies.

Figure 3.17   **The gender gap in relative performance for Economics, Social and Vocational Studies**

3.3   SUMMARY OF GCSE ENTRY PATTERNS

The analysis of examination entry data for O-levels, CSE (grade 1) and GCSE over the ten-year period reveals variation in gender entry gaps over time with an overall reduction in gender differences in patterns of entry, especially in National Curriculum subjects. What is clear is that the entry gender gap in certain subjects is so small that there is currently little difference between male and female students. Only Chemistry and Economics show an increasing entry gender gap in favour of male students; and only Social Studies shows an increasing entry gender gap in favour of female students. Mathematics and History, in contrast, demonstrate a marginally reversed gender pattern, with proportionately more girls now taking GCSE in these subjects

Table 3.1   GCSE entry patterns (1985-1994)

More Boys	Gender Gap at Entry	More Girls	Gender Gap at Entry	Change from Boys to Girls
Science	Decreasing	Biology	Decreasing	Mathematics
Chemistry	Increasing	Social Studies	Increasing	History
Physics	Decreasing	Art and Design	Decreasing	
Computer Studies	Decreasing	English Literature	Decreasing	
Technology	Decreasing	Modern Foreign Lang	Decreasing	
CDT	Decreasing	Home Economics	Decreasing	
Geography	Decreasing			
Economics	Increasing			

3.4   SUMMARY OF PUPIL PERFORMANCE IN GCSE

Subjects with higher male entries

- *Science*: the performance gender gap had, by 1994, all but disappeared but different patterns exist for the separate sciences. The entry gender gap in favour of male students has closed in Biology and Physics and whilst boys perform better in Biology, girls now perform relatively better in both Physics and Chemistry.

- *Computer Studies*: Entries remain dominated by male students but more recently female students are increasingly gaining high grades in relation to their entry.

- *Technology:* This includes traditional male (e.g. woodwork) and female (e.g. home economics) subjects. Overall it retains an entry gender gap in favour of male students, but a higher proportion of female students is currently gaining A-C grades.

- *Geography:* In 1985, there was a performance gender gap in favour of female students which has fluctuated somewhat and has risen more recently.

- *Economics:* There have been continuing entry and performance gender gaps in favour of male students but, by 1994, the performance gap reduced to almost zero.

Subjects with Higher Female Entries

- *English Language:* (where by definition there is no entry gender gap - index base of 100) The gender gap in performance in favour of female students was sustained throughout the period covered by the study.

- *Biology:* This is the only Science where female students provide the largest proportion of the entry, through they have done relatively less well than expected at A-C grades. By 1994, however, the performance gender gap had halved from the 1985 level.

- *Social Studies:* The gender gaps in favour of female students, in both entry and performance, have increased over the period of the study, with a recent small decrease in female advantage in performance.

- *Art and Design:* The entry gender gap for Art and Design is quite small, with female students gaining much better results in performance terms than could have been anticipated. Little change is evident over the period of the study.

- *English Literature*: There has continually been a gender entry gap in favour of female students but by 1994, this had become quite small. The performance gender gap in favour of female students, however, doubled in 1988 and this gap has since been maintained.

- *Modern Foreign Languages:* The relatively higher female entry in MFL has decreased over the years covered by the study. However, the increase in male entry has been paralleled by increasing female rather than male performance levels.

- *Home Economics:* As the companion subject to CDT, Home Economics has seen the entry gender gap in favour of female students decrease slightly, although their dominance in performance shows a slight increase.

Subjects with Reversals in Entry

●   *Mathematics:* In 1985, both entry and performance gender gaps favoured male students. By 1994 the entry gap had reversed marginally in favour of female students with near equality in male and female performance.

●   *History:* The gender entry gap reversed between 1985 and 1991 to produce higher female entry. From a steep improvement in performance between 1985 and 1988, female students have maintained a significant advantage in performance since 1988.

The trends in performance of students at GCSE do not provide clear evidence of the impact of the National Curriculum, especially because of its stages, and relatively recent introduction. However, the closing of the gender gap in entry, which is associated with the widening of girls' choices and entry into traditionally 'male' subject areas, and the increase of male choice and entry into traditionally 'female' subjects, appears to be partly associated with the introduction of GCSE, especially in the three years prior to the first GCSE examinations in 1988.

Female students markedly improved their performance relative to male students in Science and Mathematics after 1988, whilst in a range of other subjects, the gender gap in performance suggests a changed pattern. Factors which might have contributed to these shifts include, for example, changed curriculum content, modes of assessment, the naming and clustering of subjects, and school strategies for preparing and entering students for examinations.

3.5   GENDER PATTERNS IN SCHOOL PERFORMANCE

In 1993 the publication of GCSE results became a statutory duty. The Department for Education (DfE) has since published performance tables for all educational institutions based on their GCSE results. It is now possible to investigate the effects of type of school, *viz* girls', boys' or mixed-sex, on examination performance. For each institution, the 'league tables' give the proportion of pupils obtaining five or more Grades A-C (including starred A grades which were available for the first time in 1994). Also given are the number of pupils on roll.

Seven groupings were identified in the 1994 tables, with at least ten schools in each of the following categories: LEA Comprehensive; LEA Secondary Modern; Voluntary-aided Comprehensive; Grant-maintained Comprehensive; Grant-maintained Selective; Independent Selective; Independent with no fixed admissions policy. For each of these categories the total

Table 3.2   Proportion of pupils achieving 5+ (A-C grades) in 1994 (by school type)

	Schools	Roll	% A-C
LEA Comprehensive			
All boys	56	7,057	29.9
All girls	79	11,256	41.1
Mixed	1,804	279,279	36.3
LEA Secondary Modern			
All boys	11	1,133	18.5
All girls	16	2,160	33.8
Mixed	84	9,551	21.5
Grant-maintained Comprehensive			
All boys	43	5,842	39.7
All girls	30	3,714	50.4
Mixed	391	59,759	41.1
Grant-maintained Selective			
All boys	38	3,827	91.4
All girls	26	2,466	91.6
Mixed	23	2,209	94.0
Independent no fixed policy			
All boys	25	677	55.9
All girls	39	953	60.5
Mixed	193	3,805	57.4
Independent Selective			
All boys	119	10,542	89.6
All girls	236	12,765	91.2
Mixed	293	15,184	78.5
Voluntary-aided Comprehensive			
All boys	21	2,588	34.1
All girls	34	3,930	47.4
Mixed	255	33,893	43.4

number of pupils on roll was calculated and (by appropriate weighting) the corresponding A-to-C rates determined. These are summarised in Table 3.2.

All-girls' schools obtain higher ratings than all-boys' schools in all seven categories and were the highest performing schools in six categories. In five of the cases the mixed-sex group (which contains an unknown balance of females to males) falls midway; in the sixth case (Grant-maintained selective) mixed-sex schools gained the highest proportion of grades and in the seventh (Independent Selective) gained the lowest proportion of grades. 1994 is the only one of the four 'snapshot' years for which the performance tables are available and so it is not possible at this stage to identify trends. However, since differences found between all-boy and all-girl schools of the same category appear consistent, it is possible that gender segregation has a substantial influence on gender performance.

3.6   CONCLUSIONS

●   Gender differences in performance are found at the earliest stages of primary schooling and vary according to subject and age. Such differences suggest that attention needs to be paid to the ways in which gender patterns come to be established and how they develop within subjects over time. Early indications from pilot schemes for SATs suggest that girls perform better than boys; notably in English at Key Stage 1. By the end of Key Stage 2 boys' underachievement is particularly evident, especially in English, although proportionately more boys achieve the highest grades in Mathematics and Science.

●   SATs data have provided valuable insights into the nature and shaping of gender differences, but more monitoring and research are clearly needed to understand the effects of socio-economic status, ethnic origin, bilingualism and special needs on male and female performance patterns.

●   There has been a substantial increase in GCSE entry with female students in particular increasing their entry into the full range of subjects, including the traditionally 'male' Sciences and Mathematics. Male students have nevertheless reduced the gender entry gap in the Arts, Humanities and Languages by increasing their entry into those subjects. The entry gender gaps for most subjects are closing substantially, leaving only Chemistry, Economics and Social Studies with increasing inequality in take-up.

- Whilst female students have improved their performance in relation to entry, (especially in subjects with higher male entries) male students have not shown similar improvement in their performance over the period. They are not performing as well as might be expected from their entry figures in English, the Arts, the Humanities, Languages and Technology.

- Gender patterns in student performance may well reflect the type of school attended. Data from the school performance tables suggest that girls in single-sex schools, regardless of type, might be at a substantial advantage. However, further research is needed to clarify the relative advantages and disadvantages of single-sex and co-educational schooling.

- Changes in the patterns of GCSE entry and performance are not obviously associated with the National Curriculum. Many trends were evident prior to the implementation of the National Curriculum (from 1990 onwards) and have not been disrupted by other, more recent reforms. These include the increase in the number of qualifications at 16, the reduction in sex-divided, subject choice, the improvements in female performance. The introduction of a compulsory curriculum appears to have built upon earlier trends to broaden male and female course and subject choices, and to extend entry into traditionally gendered subject areas. Such patterns are also associated with increased female performance over and above improvements in male performance.

4 THE GENDER GAP IN SUBJECT CHOICE AND PERFORMANCE AT A-LEVEL AND IN VOCATIONAL QUALIFICATIONS

This chapter has a twin focus: on the gender gap in GCE A-level examination entry and performance and on entry and performance in vocational qualifications. GCE A-levels are regarded as the 'gold standard' and have undergone few recent revisions. In contrast vocational qualifications have been reorganised substantially into a new framework of certification.

The first section of the chapter discusses the patterns of achievement associated with school leavers and the reorganisation of vocational and academic qualifications into General National Vocational Qualifications and National Vocational Qualifications. The second section considers the patterns of gender entry and performance at A-level. Particular subjects are selected and the trends identified for the four snapshot years (1985, 1988, 1991 and 1994) chosen for the study. The final section considers gender differences in vocational qualifications.

4.1 SCHOOL LEAVERS AND CERTIFICATION

Over the last decade, as we have seen, policy makers have increasingly emphasised school performance. Currently, there are national targets for education and training and concepts of educational entitlement which encourage a closer focus upon school outcomes, particularly in relation to school leavers' qualifications. National and regional variations are also now attracting greater interest.

Additionally, the choice of qualification and preparation for work has changed substantially. Most notable of these, as we have seen, has been the introduction of the GCSE examination. Post 16, the 'gold standard' GCE A-level examination has been complemented by the new AS-level (first introduced in 1989) which students usually take at 18+. Although A- and AS-level examinations have not undergone the extent of change of 16+ examinations and syllabuses, nevertheless, the last decade has witnessed a considerable increase in the range of subjects offered at this level.

Male and female students in secondary schools and sixth form colleges can now choose from a range of academic and vocational qualifications. Since 1992, sixth form colleges have been incorporated into further education and increasingly sixth forms or their equivalents have been encouraged to offer vocational courses for students either as an alternative, or more recently, as a complement to A-level studies. School leavers, whether at 16 or 18, can study in institutions of further and higher education as well as schools, taking a range of diploma, undergraduate and postgraduate courses. In 1992, the Further and Higher Education Act granted university status to all the former polytechnics and selected colleges. Other colleges were given the right to expand their further and higher education provision.

Increasingly, more students are taking examinations. In the early 1980s, of the number of English and Welsh school leavers who left without any graded results in GCE or CSE, some successfully completed courses offered by other awarding bodies such as the Business and Technology Education Council, Royal Society of Arts (RSA), and City and Guilds London Institute (CGLI). In the course of the last ten years, provision for 16-19 year olds has been substantially reorganised. For example, in 1986, the newly established National Council for Vocational Qualifications devised a new framework of National Vocational Qualifications based on five different levels of achievement from foundation level (NVQ Level 1) to professional level (NVQ Level 5). These courses are designed to identify competence to do a particular job or a range of jobs based on clear criteria set by employers (DfE 1994a).

Many courses previously provided by schools as part of their optional course structure have been offered for NVQ accreditation. In 1991, the National Council for Vocational Qualifications also introduced General National Vocational Qualifications, which aimed to offer a general, broadly based course, preparing students for range of occupations and providing progression into higher education. By 1993, these courses had been brought into the framework for NVQs up to Level 3. Foundation and Intermediate GNVQ courses could be offered by schools to students under 16, in parallel to National Curriculum subjects. Each Advanced Level GNVQ (also taught in schools) is equivalent to two A-levels.

Previously offered in small numbers, NVQ2 and NVQ3 are currently being phased out in schools and sixth forms, having been overtaken by GNVQs. More recently, GNVQs and NVQs have been used to establish National Education and Training Targets (NETT), reflecting government concern that only approximately one third of 16-18 year olds in the United Kingdom (UK) are in full time education and training of which almost a third is part-time. Current targets[1] for the Year 2000 (revised in 1995) include:

---

[1]   Taken from NACETT 1995

Foundation learning:

- By age 19, 85 per cent of young people to achieve five GCSEs at grade C or above, an Intermediate GNVQ or an NVQ Level 2.

- 75 per cent of young people to achieve Level 2 competence in communication, numeracy and IT by age 19; and 35 per cent to achieve Level 3 competence in these core skills by age 21.

- By age 21, 60 per cent of young people to achieve two GCE A-levels, an Advanced GNVQ or an NVQ Level 3.

Lifetime learning:

- By the year 2000, 60 per cent of the workforce to be qualified to NVQ3 (or equivalent); at least two GCE A-levels, an Advanced GNVQ.

Two key trends in the pattern of qualifications of male and female school leavers over the last two decades are briefly summarised below.

Improved levels of certification of school leavers

As we have seen, between 1970 and 1989, there had been a substantial increase in the numbers of school leavers with GCSE qualifications or their equivalent. The proportion of school leavers, for example, who left school with at least one GCSE (A-C grades) or equivalent rose from 40 per cent to 60 per cent (CSO 1993) with seven out of 10 girls achieving this level in 1993.

Young women have also been more likely than young men to leave school with at least one qualification, although there are some quite substantial regional variations. For example, female students reached high levels of achievement in South East England and male students appeared to do relatively badly in regions such as Yorkshire and Humberside. Over one in six young men in Wales left school with no graded results compared with less than one in 20 in South West England (CSO 1994). Double the proportion of young women and young men in Wales than in England are likely to leave school with no graded result.

Table 4.1   School leaver's examination achievements[1] by sex and region 1990/1991

per cent

	1 + A-Level[2] SCE highers		GCSE/CSE[3]		No graded result	
	M	F	M	F	M	F
England	24.6	26.6	67.2	67.5	8.2	5.8
Wales[4]	20.8	26.9	63.2	62.8	16.0	10.3
Scotland	35.1	44.1	53.2	47.0	11.7	8.9
N Ireland	27.9	35.6	55.9	54.7	16.1	9.8

[1]   Excludes results from FE

[2]   Two AS-levels are counted as equivalent to one A-level

[3]   And equivalent grades at GCE and CSE, includes leavers with one AS-level

[4]   Includes leavers from independent schools

Source: CSO 1994, p. 51, Table 3.19

Another factor is the variation in patterns of achievement associated with men and women in particular ethnic and social groups. Adult academic achievement is lower in lower socio-economic groups and in particular ethnic groups (CSO 1993), although school leaver data does not provide an adequate base from which to assess the influence of gender on such patterns. From the national data described above, male underachievement would seem to account disproportionately for those school leavers who leave school with no graded result (over a third of school leavers in 1992 according to NACETT 1994).

In terms of A-level, the DfE Statistical Bulletin reported that, for the first time:

> *Amongst school leavers in 1991/2, a larger percentage of girls than boys gained*
> *at least one GCE A-level or equivalent - a reverse of the position in 1970/1.*
> (DfE 1994a, p. 45)

This pattern was also true for those gaining two or more A-levels. The percentage of school leavers in the UK whose highest qualification was 2+ A-levels rose from 15 per cent to 20 per cent for young.men, and from 13 per cent to 22 per cent for young women in the period between 1970/1 and 1989/90 (CSO 1993). By 1992/3, 17 per cent of young women aged 17 had achieved 3+ A-levels while at school, compared with only 15.5 per cent of similarly aged young men (DfE 1995).

Female students therefore are more likely than male students to achieve the Foundation Target (FT3) of 60 per cent of young people with at least two A-levels or equivalent (NVQ3) though there is still some way to go. In 1992/3, for example, 24.8 per cent of women reached this target compared with 20.4 per cent of men (EOC 1994). However, in relation to the earlier FT1 which targeted 80 per cent of young people to reach NVQ2, 4 per cent fewer young women than young men reached this target in 1994 although young women performed better (by about 7 per cent) than young men in achieving 5+ GCSEs (A-C grades).

According to the National Advisory Council for Education and Training Targets (NACETT 1994) this suggests that the proportion of girls achieving Level 2 vocational qualifications is about two-thirds that of boys. Thus:

> *The Council believes that further research on girls take-up of vocational qualifications is needed so that those responsible for the development of GNVQs and NVQs can take early action to address this apparent imbalance.*
> (NACETT 1994, p. 17)

Improved access to post compulsory education

In the last decade there has also been a considerable expansion of further and higher education though the period has been marked by economic recession and high unemployment. At the same time, the reorganisation both of vocational qualifications and further and higher education has been associated with new provision which appears to have brought benefits to female students in particular. Thus by 1991/2, more than two million students attended further education courses, an increase of a quarter over 1980/1.

Specifically, female students accounted for 86 per cent of the increase in further education since 1980/1981 (CSO 1994). Thus by 1991/2 women represented almost 60 per cent of all FE students; and between 1985 and 1991, the proportion of female students who entered full time further education rose from 34.9 per cent to 51.1 per cent, compared with the male equivalent of 30.5 per cent and 45.3 per cent (CSO 1993, p. 45).

Enrolments in higher education have also risen dramatically over the last ten years, reaching 1.4 million in 1992/3 (DfE 1994b). Since 1980/1, the increase in enrolments in higher education (excluding courses for nursing and paramedics) shows an increase of 99 per cent for women, compared with 33 per cent for men. Women's participation has increased to 47 per cent of the student body contrasting with 38 per cent a decade before (DfE 1994b). Female university students trebled in the period between 1970 and 1991, especially in the new universities.

Hence, by 1992, women had nearly caught up with men in the enrolment to full-time degrees - 602,000 compared with 695,000 - representing an increase in the proportion of women in every sector of higher education. Female part-time students in education increased eight fold in the last 20 years (linked to a rise in mature women students).

In contrast with such breaking down of gender inequalities in entry to further and higher education, patterns of course choice remain more entrenched. Official data illustrate the continuing separation between male and female course choices in the post compulsory sector, seen most acutely in universities. In 1989/90 for example, some 46 per cent of male students studied Science or Engineering compared with 26 per cent of women. The higher the level of the qualification, the sharper the gender gap in course entry in relation to these two spheres (DfE et al. 1992, 1993).

4.2   DEFINING THE GENDER GAP FOR A-LEVELS

Over the ten year period the proportion of the age cohort (16 - 18 year olds) now taking A-levels has changed significantly - a rise of approximately 12 per cent. The male cohort has risen from just over 73,000 in 1985, to just under 78,500 in 1994, although a low point was reached in 1988 when the figures dipped below 70,000. Female cohort sizes have shown a similar pattern, reducing from just under 67,500 in 1985 to 64,270 in 1988 and then just over 87,500 in 1994.

Not surprisingly, therefore, the rise in numbers of young women choosing A-levels has been far steeper than that for young men, so that by 1994 females outnumber males by over 9,000. These cohort sizes have been used as the basis for indexing A-levels. Thus the analysis which follows applies to the (estimated) Year 13 cohort in the four snapshot years (see Appendix A for more details of the framework used).

Students' choice of subjects has also changed, shifting from Mathematics and Sciences towards the Social Sciences. A fundamental difference between GCSE and A-level lies in the nature of the choice involved. Post-16, not only is there more choice of institution (e.g. school sixth forms, sixth form colleges or colleges of further education), but also more choice of subjects.

A variety of subjects is usually on offer from which a small number (usually three or four) will be chosen. There is no core curriculum (although many centres insist on some common non A-level participation) and students are often free to attend as they choose.

The project study focused on performances at A-level in the higher grades (A/B) with the depiction of the gender performance gap following the same analysis as presented in Chapter 3. The same sign convention applies so that (+) values indicate a better than expected female performance and (-) values indicate a better than expected male performance. The size of each gender gap is provided on the Appendix.

4.3   GENDER GAPS AT A-LEVEL

The following figures present graphically the gender gap in student choices and performance for those subject areas where the numbers are sufficiently large for any changes to show.

Mathematics, Science and Technology

Figure 4.1   A-Level Mathematics entry

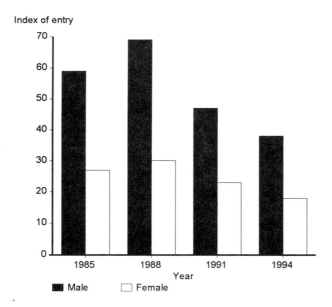

Mathematics showed a steady decline in A-level entries over the period, although there was a slight upward turn in 1988. Although Figure 4.1 provides data on entries for all Mathematics examinations, the trends for specific constituents are largely similar.

Since 1988, male patterns of entry have been parallelled by those of female entry with the trend currently downwards for both sexes and little evidence of a proportionate reduction in the gender gap with approximately two to one male to female students. Young women remain much less likely than young men to enter Mathematics A-level.

Figure 4.2   The gender gap in relative performance for Mathematics

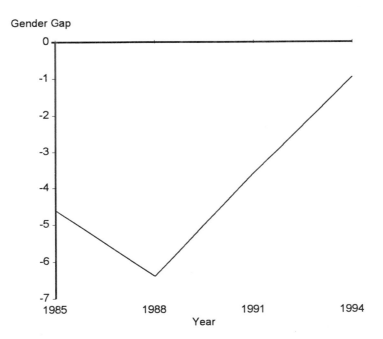

Although it can be seen from Figure 4.1 that Mathematics A-level entries have continued to drop since 1988, it is clear from Figure 4.2 that there has been a substantial rise in the proportion of female students obtaining higher grades given their proportion of the entry. Part of this change might be attributed to the introduction of modular courses, which, in 1994, accounted for about a third of the Mathematics entry. A-level subjects and courses are gradually being modularised and Mathematics is the first subject in which such schemes have become firmly established. However, the increase in entry to such schemes has not been sufficient to offset the decline in entry in the traditional Mathematics syllabuses. Changes in entry patterns, and in performance of the two types of syllabus are complex and appear unpredictable.

51

The majority of Science entries continue in the separate sciences of Biology, Chemistry and Physics, and to present them as a cluster (as has been done at GCSE) would disguise the most important differences. They are therefore presented separately as follows:

Figure 4.3   **A-Level Science entry**

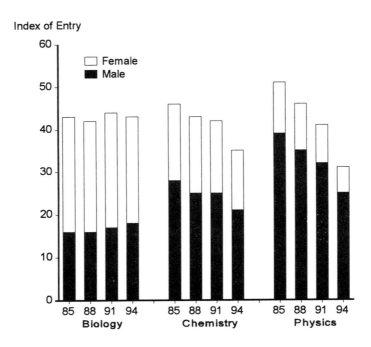

In Figure 4.3 it is clear that gender pattern of entry varies for the different sciences. Biology has been more popular with young women throughout the period of study, with entries for both sexes remaining fairly stable over the ten year period, for males especially so. In Chemistry there has been a decline in the predominately male entry, while for females the entry has been largely stable, though declining more recently.

Physics has the biggest entry gender gap, with young men predominating, though it is also noticeable that from 1985 there has been a steadily declining take-up of this subject by both sexes. These results offer a sharp contrast with the GCSE experience. Interestingly, there was no marked peaking in any Science in 1991, the first year in the study when follow-through from change emanating from Year 11 GCSE examinations was most likely to be seen. It would appear that the shifting entry gap for GCSE Sciences has not transferred to A-level Sciences. The entry gender gap in favour of female students in Biology can be seen to have narrowed slightly. In contrast, the entry gender gap in favour of male students for Physics has increased (from 54 per cent in 1985 to 60 per cent in 1994).

Figure 4.4   **The gender gap in relative performance for the Sciences**

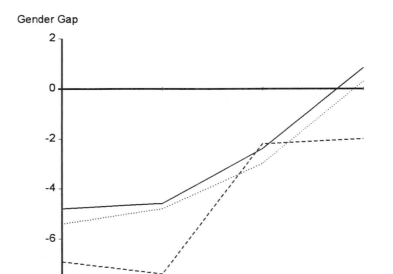

The patterns of performance are different for each of the Sciences and demonstrate the considerable variability in the gender gap over time. For Biology, which uniquely for the Sciences has a higher entry of female students, the gender performance gap in favour of male students had disappeared by 1994.

Conversely there is, and has always been, a greater than expected proportion of young men gaining high grades in Physics and Chemistry, though this has varied considerably throughout the ten-year period. Although the entry gender gap in Physics in favour of male students has increased since 1985, there is now no gender gap in relation to performance. There is also evidence of a considerable narrowing of the performance gender gap in Chemistry.

Technology contains subjects which appear largely sex-stereotyped. For example, Home Economics has a low male entry and CDT has an equivalently low female entry. Young women appear to be considerably less likely to enter Technology subjects than they did in 1985. This may be linked to the much steeper increase in the take-up of CDT by young men. When the data

53

is indexed against a rising student population, the female entry has reduced slightly whereas male entries have risen slightly. Taken together, the entry gender gap for Technology in favour of male students has clearly increased (from 18 per cent in 1984 to 47 per cent in 1994).

Figure 4.5   **A-Level Technology entry**

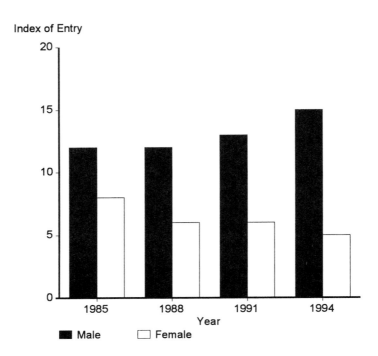

Despite the increase in male entries since 1985, the performance gap in favour of male students in Technology, as given in Figure 4.6, has shifted to show the increasing success of young women. The trend in the gender gap apparent in this figure derives from the increasing male entry and a lower proportion of that entry gaining a grade A or B; resulting since 1991 in signs of a decreasing male higher level of performance.

Also, Computer Studies, a fringe subject allied to Technology, shows a similar entry gender gap, holding constant at a ratio of five male to one female students and showing little change over the years covered by the study. Although male subjects performed well in the subject, this advantage has been decreasing over the period.

Figure 4.6   **The gender gap in relative performance for Technology subjects**

English and Modern Foreign Languages

The English figures are an amalgamation of those subjects called English, English Literature and Language, with Modern Foreign Languages encompassing all foreign languages (including Welsh) set at A-level, but dominated by French, and to a lesser extent German.

As can be seen from Figure 4.7, an entry gender gap in favour of female students has continued over the ten-year period but with a reduction in the gap over the years (from 44 per cent in 1984 to 34 per cent in 1994). Figure 4.8 below illustrates performance in English and Modern Foreign Languages.

This figure illustrates the frequent assertion that, though a minority entry in the language subjects at A-level, young men perform better in the top grades. It would, however, appear that the gender performance gap is decreasing in Modern Foreign Languages. Higher male performance in relation to entry in English has also decreased more recently and is currently almost zero.

Figure 4.7   **A-Level Language entry**

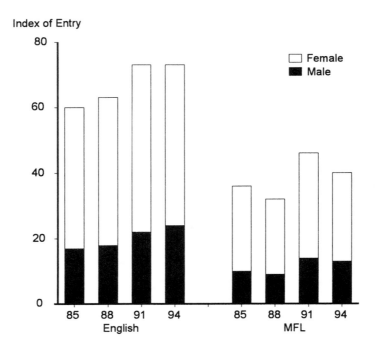

Figure 4.8   **The gender gap in relative performance for English and Modern Foreign Languages**

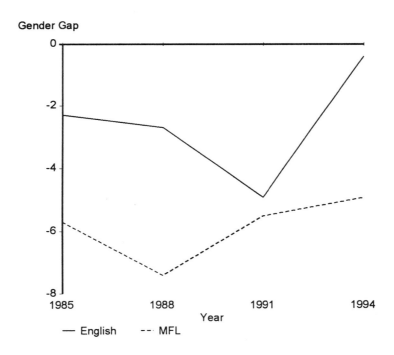

Humanities and the Arts

The pattern of entry for Geography and History for the two sexes is clearly different. In History there are proportionately more women, and in Geography more men, but the entry gender gap in both subjects appears to be closing. However, young men's higher entry in Geography appears to have been relatively stable between 1985 and 1994, with 1991 as the year with the narrowest entry gender gap (see Figure 4.9 below).

Figure 4.9   A-Level Geography and History entries

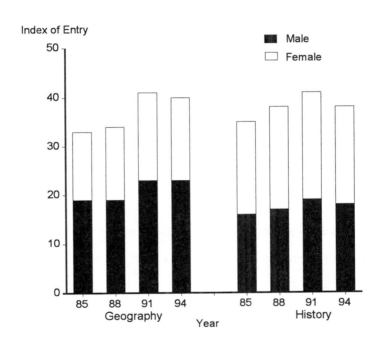

History has had a performance gender gap in favour of male students which has nevertheless reduced over time. In Figure 4.10 performance in History is contrasted with that for Geography, a subject which is more popular with young men, but in which young women are increasingly gaining a larger proportion of the top grades.

Although the change (i.e. gradient) in the gender gap is similar for both humanities subjects, indicating a continuing increase in the performance of young women, young men continue to gain a higher proportion of the top History grades than could be anticipated from their entry, and young women, a minority sex for Geography, are similarly gaining more high grades than could be expected. Also worthy of note is how the trends in the two subjects closely mirror each other so that male advantage in History is decreasing at the same rate as the female advantage in Geography is increasing.

Figure 4.10   **The gender gap in relative performance for History and Geography**

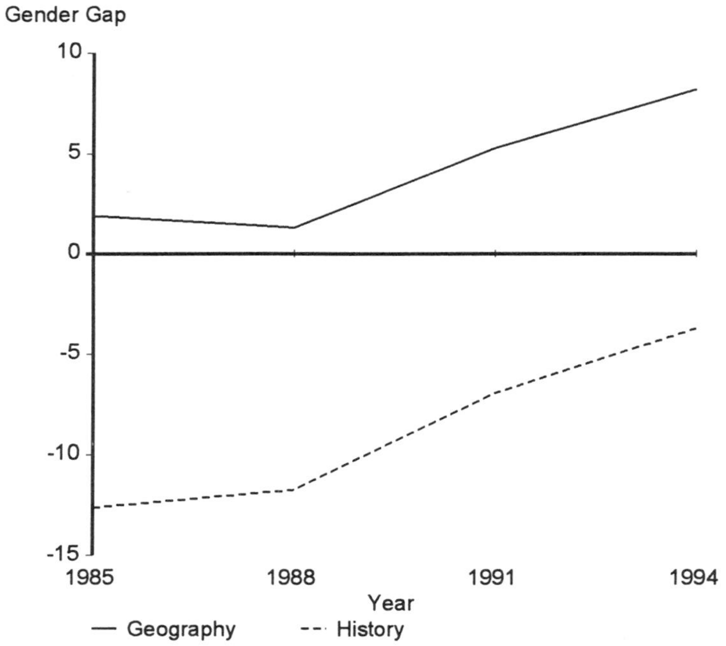

As can be seen in Figure 4.11, Art (and Art and Design) has a strong entry gender gap in favour of female students, with young women taking up two-thirds of the entry. More recently the proportion of female entry has begun to decline, however, while male entry has shown a steady, if slight, increase.

The gender performance gap in favour of male students reduced substantially between 1988 and 1991, the year when female entry began to fall, as can be seen in Figure 4.12. The change of direction was sustained in 1994 with the gender gap showing that female students now perform better than male students relative to their entry.

Social Sciences

Economics is the largest entry subject of all the Social Sciences. Its entry gender gap in favour of male students is illustrated in Figure 4.13 below, and contrasted with that of Social Studies (an amalgam of small entry subjects of which the largest is Sociology) which has almost doubled in numbers over the period. The entry gender gap in Social Studies has remained fairly constant (approximately 24.5 per cent) with young women continuing their high entry to the subject. In contrast, the entry gender gap for Economics is increasing, with more young men choosing it as a subject of study. However, overall numbers are declining for this subject.

58

Figure 4.11   **A-Level Art and Design entry**

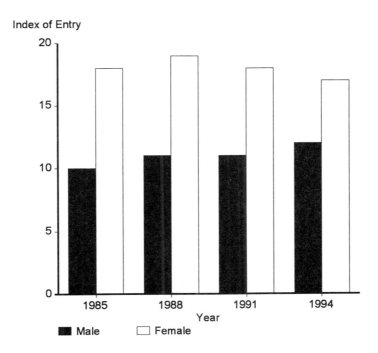

Figure 4.12   **The gender gap in relative performance for Art and Design**

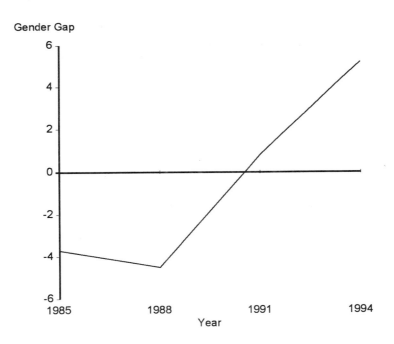

Social Sciences

Economics is the largest entry subject of all the Social Sciences. Its entry gender gap in favour of male students is illustrated in Figure 4.13 below, and contrasted with that of Social Studies (an amalgam of small entry subjects of which the largest is Sociology) which has almost doubled in numbers over the period. The entry gender gap in Social Studies has remained fairly constant (approximately 24.5 per cent) with young women continuing their high entry to the subject. In contrast, the entry gender gap for Economics is increasing, with more young men choosing it as a subject of study. However, overall numbers are declining for this subject.

Figure 4.13   **A-Level Economics and Social Studies entries**

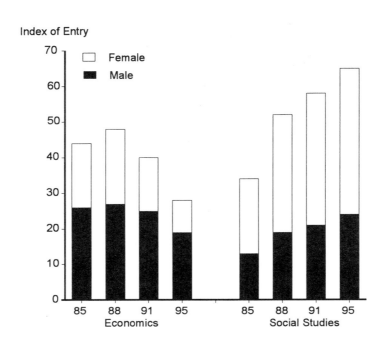

Economics has continued to produce a gender performance gap in favour of young men, a trend that nevertheless sharply decreased in 1988. Social Studies performance has been rather more inconsistent; with young men gaining a higher than expected proportion of top grades in 1985, relative equity in 1988, higher performance in 1991, and in 1994, a reverse of the trend with a gender performance gap emerging in favour of young women. However, the scale of these fluctuations is small compared with changes in the gender gap for other subjects.

Student entry into Business Studies has risen steadily, with a slightly steeper increase of male students. Entry to Psychology has also increased but in this case the rise is much steeper for female students. Law too has seen an increase in popularity, but here there has been little gender difference in take-up. In contrast, Political Studies, which had similar entries for each sex in 1985, has seen a decrease in female entry such that young men now account for nearly twice as many entries as young women. Thus the overall picture for these subjects is inconsistent.

Figure 4.14   **The gender gap in relative performance for Economics and Social Studies**

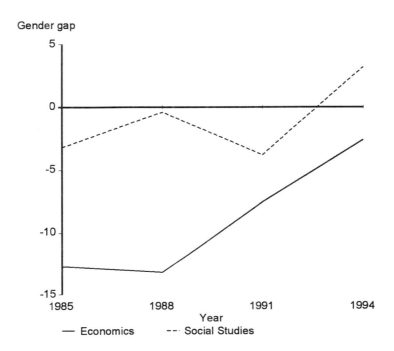

Other subjects, for example the Classics, Creative Arts, Vocational Studies, Physical Education (PE) and Drama, show little difference in entry either between sexes or over time. The exception is that of Communication Studies, first registering entries in 1991, where young women account for nearly twice as many of the entries as young men. The only other subject large enough to register indexed entries and performance is General Studies, where there has been considerable stability over the years showing male entry to be slightly higher (about two per cent) than female entry and with male students performing better than female students.

4.4   SUMMARY OF GENDER ENTRIES AT A-LEVEL

Many A-level subjects continue to show a clear gender gap in entry. Table 4.2 below lists subjects and the gender gaps in entries throughout the ten year period covered by the study.

A-levels with higher male entries have tended to show increased entry in favour of males, except for Chemistry and Mathematics which have shown little change. In contrast, A-levels which conventionally have had higher female entry have shown male entry patterns moving closer to those of females. Young women have increased proportionally (in entry terms) only in Social Studies.

Table 4.2   **Changes in A-Level entry 1985-1994**

Higher Male Entry	Gender Gap	Higher Female Entry	Gender Gap
Chemistry	No change	Biology	Decreasing
Physics	Increasing	Art and Design	Decreasing
Mathematics	No change	History	Decreasing
Geography	Increasing	Social Studies	Increasing
Economics	Increasing	English[1]	Decreasing
Technology	Increasing	Modern Foreign Lang	Decreasing
Computer Studies	Increasing		

[1]   In 1985 the title English referred to English Literature; from 1988 onwards it referred to an amalgamation of English Literature and Language.

4.5   SUMMARY OF GENDER PERFORMANCE AT A-LEVEL

Subjects with higher male entries

● *Science:* Although Science subjects overall have seen the performance gender gap disappear over the time frame, more interesting is the pattern of the separate sciences (still chosen in preference to 'Science', though the latter is becoming more popular at A-level). In 1985, in both Chemistry and Physics, young men accounted for more high performances than their entry would suggest but by 1994, this had reduced to a more equal balance in performance between the sexes.

● *Mathematics:* The entry gender gap has remained stable, though there has been a similar change in performance to that in Science, with female students performing more recently at similar levels to male students.

● *Geography:* Whilst the entry gender gap has not changed, female higher performance has become more marked.

- *Economics:* The entry gender gap in favour of males has continued to increase. However, by 1994 the performance gender gap in favour of male students had substantially narrowed.

- *Technology:* There has been little change in entry and performance gender gaps until 1994, though both have increased over the time span, and taken together they indicate a narrowing in the performance gender gap favouring male students.

- *CDT:* The pattern for Economics is repeated for CDT where an increasing entry gender gap has not been accompanied by a parallel increase in higher male performance.

- *Computer Studies:* The entry gender gap for computer studies remains stable, although by 1994 female students had increased their level of performance in the subject relative to male students.

Subjects with higher female entries

- *Biology:* Female students have tended to perform less well in Biology despite the entry gender gap in their favour. In 1994 this pattern had reduced to a more equitable balance in performance between the sexes.

- *Art and Design:* Although there has been a gender gap in performance in favour of male students, this has been reversed in recent years such that, by 1994, female students had increased their proportion of higher grade levels.

- *History:* By 1994, the high female entry had much reduced. Similarly, female students' relatively poorer performance showed substantial improvement.

- *Social Studies:* Although Social Studies has seen the biggest overall rise in entries in recent years, gender performance gaps have fluctuated throughout the ten-year period and currently female performance appears to be on an upward curve.

- *English:* Conventionally, young women have entered in greater numbers and young men have gained the highest grades. However, entry and performance gender gaps have closed over the ten-year period and currently both sexes produce similar levels of performance.

- *Modern Foreign Languages:* MFL has a similar pattern to that for English, except that over the years there has been a less marked decline in male students' proportion of the higher grades.

63

A-level data suggest that despite variations in the entry gender gap, there have been relatively few substantial changes. However, there has been a reduction in the relatively higher performance of male students since 1985, and in two subject areas - Social Studies and Art and Design - there has been a reversal in performance trends in favour of young women.

The sex segregation of subjects at A-level is still clearly reflected in entry patterns with some subjects increasingly associated with male students (e.g. Geography, Economics, Technology and Computer Studies). Such patterns contrast with those found at GCSE, and do not have an obvious link to the National Curriculum, suggesting that factors other than success in gaining a pass in a subject are implicated in course choice and performance between 16 and 18.

4.6   THE GENDER GAP IN VOCATIONAL QUALIFICATIONS

Little official information is currently available on gender patterns in course choice and performance for vocational qualifications. However, a recent research report provides useful information on the gender gap in such qualifications. Felstead, Goodwin and Green (1995) conducted a study of women's attainment of vocational qualifications (up to and including the age of 21) based on data from the Quarterly Labour Force Survey (QLFS 1994) and the National Information System for Vocational Qualifications (NISVQ). The data base included Scotland as well as England, Wales and Northern Ireland.

Felstead et al. demonstrated that in relation to Foundation Target 3, the gender performance gap in vocational qualifications was greater than that for academic qualifications. Young women under 21 were more likely than young men to achieve at least two A-levels or equivalent, but less likely to achieve specific vocational qualifications (e.g. RSA, BTEC, City-Guilds Advanced Craft).

Such gender gaps have also been affected by national variations. The analysis of Felstead et al. shows that the gender gap in favour of male attainment in vocational qualifications in Wales was greater than for the UK as a whole; in England it was 7.5 per cent compared with 10.5 per cent in Wales. Table 4.4 also shows the extent to which gender gaps in academic and vocational qualifications vary by ethnic origin.

Table 4.3   Foundation Target 3: Type of qualification and gender [1]

per cent

Type of Qualification	All	Male	Female	Gender Gap (Male - Female)
Vocational Qualifications	432,772 (17.4)	269,791 (21.3)	162,931 (13.4)	7.9
Academic Qualifications	542,522 (21.8)	275,132 (21.7)	267,390 (21.9)	-0.2
All Qualifications	975,243 (39.2)	544,923 (43.0)	430,321 (35.3)	7.7

[1]   For up to 21-year old men and women in the UK

Source: adapted from Felstead et al. (1995) calculations based on QLFS, Spring 1994, ref Table 3.13, p. 38)

Table 4.4   Foundation Target 3: Academic and vocational qualifications by ethnic origin and gender

per cent

Ethnic Origin	Vocational		Gender Gap	Academic		Gender Gap
	M	F	Male-Female	M	F	Male-Female
White	21.6	13.5	8.1	20.7	22.3	-1.6
Black	27.4	22.0	5.4	18.3	14.4	3.9
Indian	18.2	28.1	-9.9	30.8	24.9	5.9
Pakistani/Bangladeshi	19.9	4.8	15.1	12.5	13.5	-1.0
Mixed/Other origins	19.3	8.1	11.2	31.6	18.9	12.7

1   For up to 21-year old men and women

Source: Felstead et al. (1995) Tables 3.18 and 3.19, p. 41 calculated from QLFS

For most ethnic groups, young men gain more vocational qualifications than young women. The gender gap is substantial within the white population, amongst Black men and women and particularly acute within Pakistani/Bangladeshi groups and those categorised as having 'mixed/other origins'. In contrast, higher proportions of academic qualifications are found amongst white and Pakistani /Bangladeshi women than men. Noticeably more women than men of Indian origin acquire vocational qualifications and more men in this category acquire academic qualifications.

Interestingly, no marked differences in the gender gap in vocational qualifications were found in relation to social class. The greatest differences were amongst those in intermediate occupations (routine work) with a gender gap of 7.7 per cent in favour of men, and in the armed forces where the gender gap was 19.5 per cent.

Felstead et al. also considered the pattern of achievement of young men and women under the age of 18. They compared NVQ qualifications with non-NVQ (traditional vocational courses) in 1991/2 and 1992/3 using data from NISVQ. For 1991/2 overall they found a greater proportion of awards were made to men at Levels 3, 4, and 5, with nearly half (49.6 per cent) of young men aged 18 achieving Level 3 or above, compared with 37.2 per cent of 18-year old women.

The gender gap in non-NVQ courses also showed that women were less likely to take these courses and, when they did, they were less likely to achieve Levels 3, 4, and 5 (this was less marked for younger age groups).

Female vocational qualifications were more likely to involve NVQ courses (although the numbers were still small). Here the data for 1991/2 showed that women achieved two-thirds of all NVQs, usually at Levels 3, 4, and 5.

The data for 1992/3 showed some change (affected perhaps by the inclusion of NVQs in schools). The gender gap had narrowed for young men and women in relation to Level 3 awards (two A-level equivalents). Women had increased their share of Level 2 non-NVQ awards even though the proportion taking these courses was still well behind that for men (40 per cent women compared to 57 per cent men).

Young men were more likely to achieve 'traditional' vocational qualifications and young women were more likely to take the 'new' vocational qualifications. Such patterns reflected what was termed a 'strong gender bias' since:

> *only a small percentage of qualifications related to male dominated occupations were awarded to women. However, there were signs that the pattern was less pronounced for the new qualifications.*
> (Felstead et al. 1995, p. 55)

Vocational programmes and awards play a key role in preparing students for access into higher level qualifications. Of great concern, therefore, is not merely the completion rate and the level of award achieved of importance, but also the pattern of course choice.

BTEC course choices

Bailey's (1992) study of student non-completion of BTEC programmes and awards offers a more detailed insight into recent gender gaps in course choice and completion rates. The research found that:

- The gender breakdown of BTEC programmes is generally along traditional lines but with a slow increase in the small proportion of female students in Engineering, Construction and Computing programmes.

- The proportion of female students in Science programmes is high, however, they are mainly found in conventionally feminine areas of study such as Beauty, Caring, Caring Services (Nursery Nursing; Social Care), and Science (Dental Assisting; Health Studies; Applied Biology).

- A gender gap in favour of male students can be found in conventionally masculine subject areas such as Industrial Technology, Physics, Chemistry and increasingly, Music Technology and Musical Instrument Technology.

- Award programmes entitled 'Science' show a more balanced intake though with more males on Diplomas at all levels.

- A number of specialised programmes at Higher National Certificate (HNC) level have an entry gender gap in favour of female students, e.g. Science (Medical Laboratory, Medical Physics and Physiological Measurement, Pharmaceutical, Applied Biology).

In Business and Finance courses and programmes female students have tended to predominate at First Certificate level, but this is gradually being eroded. The achievement gender gap has also reversed in favour of male students gaining the First Diploma (Bailey 1992).

BTEC course completion

Female students appear to be doing well in terms of completion rates on BTEC courses. Analysis shows that more female students have been achieving completions proportional to their share of registrations. As Bailey argues, 'all things being equal' one would expect that each sex would achieve a proportion of certificates that matched the proportion of registrations. The data were thus analysed in terms of the comparative achievement of male and female students for different levels of award, in different subject areas over the period 1987/8 to 1990/1. The following gender gaps in course completion were found:

- *Agriculture:* Proportionately more female students achieve awards, particularly on the National Certificate (+8 per cent), but fewer gain a National Diploma (-11 per cent).

- *Business and Finance:* Female achievement has been consistently higher across all levels (between +6 per cent and +8 per cent).

- *Computing and Information Systems:* Female achievement is higher at Ordinary National Certificate (ONC) (+13 per cent), with equity in male and female achievement across National Diploma and HNC levels.

- *Construction:* Although very small numbers of female students took this subject, they were found to achieve a slightly higher proportion of awards than male students (between +1 per cent to 4 per cent), except at HNC where males had higher achievement levels (-4 per cent).

- *Service Industries:* Proportionally more female students achieved qualifications than male students across all levels (between +5 per cent and +11 per cent).

- *Engineering:* Though few young women took this subject, female students achieved comparable levels of success at First Certificate and HNC, and more awards at First Diploma (+4 per cent) and ONC (+1 per cent), but did not do as well as males at National Diploma level (-7 per cent).

- *Public Administration:* Female students achieved better results than their male counterparts in this subject area (ONC +13 per cent, National Diploma +18 per cent, and HNC +9 per cent).

- *Science and Caring:* Male and females students performed almost identically, with young women doing particularly well, however, at First Diploma level (+18 per cent).

The only Board for which female students did not achieve as high a proportion of awards as male students was *Design*. Bailey found that:

> *at National Certificate level, National Diploma and Higher National Diploma (HND) levels male and female achievement is comparable, but at First Certificate, First Diploma and HNC levels female students achieved significantly*

less well than males proportionately (-16 per cent, -3 per cent and -9 per cent respectively).
(Ibid. p. 43)

Of the 158 cohort results for 1987/8, 128 show more positive results for female students; only 29 showed male student completion rates higher than for women and ten reported equal completion rates. The study also reveals that: 'the Boards where women did particularly well are those with a large preponderance of female candidates (Business and Finance, Science and Caring, Public Administration.)'. (Ibid. p. 45)

Where female students were in a minority, the pattern of success differed: in Agriculture they did less well; in Computing young women did as well or better than young men (although not at National Diploma); the small group of female students in Construction did as well or better than male students; in Engineering young women achieved as well or better than young men; and on the Design Board, where there are more males, female students achieved levels nearly equal to those of male students.

Summary

Although there is evidence (from BTEC) that young women have relatively high completion rates, otherwise, young men are on the whole, more likely to obtain vocational qualifications and these are often at a higher level. The gender gaps in relation to vocational qualifications are much wider than for academic qualifications, although they may be narrowing with the introduction of new vocational courses and pathways. Course choice patterns, however, still suggest gendered routes into occupational spheres, with slow progress being made in breaking down gender divisions.

4.7   CONCLUSIONS

- The ten-year period covered by the study is associated with a considerable rise in achievement of all compulsory and post compulsory qualifications, especially amongst young women. School leavers' data suggest that although young women leave school more qualified than young men, there are important national, regional, ethnic and social differences in gender patterns. Gender differences amongst those who leave school with no graded qualifications, it is suggested, need further investigation.

- Gender differences continue to remain in relation to subject entry. Although young men are closing the gap in relation to a number of A-level subjects in the Humanities, young women have not reduced the entry gender gap in most of the Sciences. Young men are increasing their entry advantage in subjects such as Physics and Computer Studies and maintaining the entry gender gap in Chemistry and Mathematics. This would suggest that effort needs to be directed towards reducing such gender differences in the Sciences.

- There has been a marked improvement in performance of female students in almost all subjects at A-level, especially those where male students have tended to be over-represented in entries. In 1985, male students gained a majority of high performances in all subject areas except Geography. By 1994, this performance advantage had reduced considerably, sometimes to a position of relative equity, and occasionally (for example in Social Studies and Art and Design) to a position where female students were producing better performance levels than their male counterparts.

- The data on gender patterns of course choice and performance in vocational qualifications is incomplete. However, the research reveals the importance of monitoring gender performance and, in particular, the effects of locality, ethnicity, and differences in level of qualification. The setting of national education and training targets and the new frameworks for GNVQs for schools suggest that such data could usefully be brought into line with examination board data at national level, providing a basis for more effective gender monitoring of performance in schools.

- Young women appear to have greater success in completing vocational courses even when in a minority; but there remains a considerable gender gap in favour of male students in the achievement of vocational qualifications, particularly among certain ethnic groups. Gender continues to influence the selection of courses, such that young women and men continue to choose different qualifications with particular gendered occupational implications.

5 EDUCATIONAL REFORM, EQUAL OPPORTUNITIES AND CHANGING LEA-SCHOOL RELATIONS

This chapter focuses on the interrelationships between educational reform and LEA - school relations, especially the support provided by LEAs for equal opportunities developments in primary and secondary schools in England and Wales. Evidence for the nature of this support and how it might have changed, both from the LEA and schools' point of view, was collected from the surveys and visits to local authorities and schools.

A key aspect of the Education Reform Act 1988 was the introduction of local management of schools with the consequent redistribution of financial, organisational, administrative and educational planning from LEAs to school governing bodies. Special attention therefore is focused upon the effects this might have had upon the development of school equal opportunities policies and practices.

Further, the creation of a new system of regular school inspections by OFSTED could also have particular significance for the promotion of equal opportunities in schools. A key question, therefore, was to discover the extent to which the new forms of inspection might trigger equal opportunities initiatives as part of school improvement. The experience of schools which had already been inspected provided interesting insights into the possibilities of OFSTED to promote what might be termed 'equality assurance'.

The first section of this chapter describes briefly the context for the evidence collected from LEAs and schools. The second section considers the extent of equal opportunities policy-making: the impetus for reform, policy coverage and the extent of school commitment to such issues. The third section investigates LEAs' views of their influence on equal opportunities policies and practices in schools and the extent to which this has changed. Schools also reported on current LEA services and how they supported equal opportunities work.

The fourth section considers past and current commitment of LEAs, in particular, to monitor equal opportunities in schools and provide equal opportunities training for teachers and governors; whilst the final section focuses attention on the role of OFSTED in equal opportunities work.

71

5.1   THE POLICY CONTEXT

A number of factors affect any attempt to assess the changing role of LEAs in relation to equal opportunities work in schools. These include:

- *Defining Equal Opportunities*: The terms equal opportunities and gender equality (as discussed in Chapter 2) have been defined in a variety of ways. The meanings attached to such concepts affect how existing LEA and school practice is understood by those working within such institutions. What for some schools might seem a failure to tackle equality issues in another context might be reported as 'active' engagement with the issues. Also, what is meant by an equal opportunities policy can range from a brief note in a prospectus to a full document with a clearly defined implementation strategy. (Chapter 7 explores some current understandings in more detail.)

- *Equal Opportunities Focus*: For some schools and local authorities, gender equality may refer exclusively to gender issues; whilst in other contexts it is combined with issues such as class, disability, race, ethnicity, bilingualism, sexuality etc.

- *Past Levels of Provision*: The extent to which recent reforms have affected LEAs' ability to support equal opportunities in schools is dependent to a considerable extent upon the level of provision in the past. There has always been wide diversity in the range of services offered by LEAs both to support equal opportunities initiatives and in the methods used to encourage developments at school level. The scale of investment, both financial and personal, differs considerably both in the past and in the current climate. Without such information, the data provided by surveys and interviews at best offer only a partial analysis of national provision.

- *Introduction of Local Management of Schools (LMS)*: This key reform significantly altered the balance of the relationship between LEAs and schools. Before LMS, LEAs had the main responsibility for the provision of education for all children in their locality. This involved many LEAs in promoting initiatives, supporting teachers' practice and school policy development in the area of equal opportunities. Since the advent of LMS, this overall LEA role has disappeared. Schools now have responsibility for ensuring equal entitlement for all their pupils and, therefore, have the choice of whom to approach for any advice and support.

- *Local Impact of the Reforms*: LEAs have experienced the impact of the reforms in different ways. In some authorities, the reforms have meant a considerable cutting back of services, especially if a significant number of schools have opted out of authority control. The ways in which LMS has been introduced have also been affected by prior LEA-school relations and also by how local councils have chosen to develop new partnership relationships with schools. In some areas, LEA provision for equal opportunities was always low key; for others, the introduction of LMS was likely to constrain the ability to retain existing levels of support and advice to schools. The yardstick by which the effects of the reforms on the role of LEAs in promoting equal opportunities can be measured will therefore differ considerably depending on this past context.

Further, as LEAs struggle to maintain their role in local educational planning, the extent to which individuals, whether at LEA or school level, might 'over-report' activity in this area must also be taken into consideration. The tension between the schools' view and LEAs' view of the services provided locally is therefore of particular interest.

Given such concerns it is important to take into account the source of the data presented here and in later chapters (see also Chapter 1). The LEA survey data, which was collected from 49 English and three Welsh LEAs - a total of 52 LEAs, was supplied by a wide range of personnel, several of whom were Chief Education Officers (CEOs)/Directors of Education. The majority of respondents saw themselves as having special responsibility for equal opportunities. Approximately nine out of 10 primary school respondents from the 390 Welsh and English primary schools surveyed were headteachers; the rest were mainly deputy, or assistant deputy, heads. In contrast, secondary school respondents (from 223 English and 12 Welsh schools), tended to be teachers with special responsibility for equal opportunities; a third were headteachers.

Significantly for the purposes of this research, the majority of English LEA respondents had been appointed by the authority relatively recently, with 40 per cent having worked for the LEA for ten years or more and 30 per cent having worked for the authority for less than four years.

Thirty per cent of English primary and secondary school survey respondents had worked in the school for more than nine years. This provided a contrast with the 43 per cent of primary and 63 per cent of secondary school respondents in Wales.

When asked, proportionately more Welsh primary and secondary school respondents (approximately 44 per cent and 43 per cent respectively) than their English colleagues (approximately 38 per cent and 33 per cent respectively) reported being involved in equal opportunities before 1989. To some extent, therefore, more of the Welsh school respondents would be in a better position to observe the effects of reforms in the last ten years, since there seems to have been less staff turnover. The majority (50-60 per cent) of school responses to the survey came from those who had, on the whole, become involved in equal opportunities after the Education Reform Act.

5.2   EQUAL OPPORTUNITIES POLICY DEVELOPMENT

In 1988 the Equal Opportunities Commission (EOC) surveyed English and Welsh LEAs to discover whether there were in existence specialist policies, special responsibility posts or specialist working groups on gender equality. Over half (56 per cent) of English LEAs reported then that they had an equal opportunities policy or statement referring to gender; and another 27.5 per cent that they had plans to adopt an equal opportunities policy. 16.5 per cent reported no such plans. The majority of LEAs had already developed, it seemed at the time, policy statements on gender or were planning to do so. (EOC 1988, p. 6-7)

Six years later, the pattern of LEA responses to similar questions had changed considerably. Two per cent of the LEAs surveyed for the project reported having neither a policy covering gender nor an equal opportunities policy which included gender. Two-thirds of the English and Welsh LEAs had specialist policy statements on gender (but only one out of the three Welsh LEAs). Three-quarters of the English and Welsh LEAs had both a policy statement on gender *and* an equal opportunities policy which specifically included gender; and 24 per cent did not have a specialist gender policy but had included gender in a broader policy statement on equal opportunities.

Table 5.1 below shows how many LEAs and schools have equal opportunities policies, how many are still developing them and what proportion of these policies include gender.

Table 5.1   **Policies on equal opportunities which include gender**

per cent

	LEAs			Primary Schools			Secondary Schools		
	E	W	E&W	E	W	E&W	E	W	E&W
Yes	98	100	98	82	68	81	94	73	93
No	2	—	2	2	5	2	1	—	—
Currently Being Drafted	—	—	—	17	27	17	6	27	7
N	49	3	52	359	31	390	223	12	235

The majority of primary and secondary schools in the English and Welsh surveys reported having an equal opportunities policy which included gender, whilst 17 per cent of English primary schools, six per cent of English secondary schools and 27 per cent of both Welsh primary and secondary schools were still in the process of drafting such a statement. 90 per cent of English secondary schools (and 89 per cent of CTCs) in the study had already developed such policies.

In the majority of English and Welsh LEAs and schools, the equal opportunities policies being referred to by respondents were of relatively recent origin, having being introduced in the last five years. Approximately 40 per cent of LEAs in the English survey introduced an equal opportunities policy in 1989 (a year after the Education Reform Act), 20 per cent of the secondary schools in the sample did likewise in 1990, whilst 38 per cent of primary schools in England and Wales did not produce policies until 1992.

Table 5.2   **Date of introduction of equal opportunities policies by LEAs and schools**

per cent

	LEAs			Primary Schools			Secondary Schools		
	E	W	E&W	E	W	E&W	E	W	E&W
Pre 1989	39	—	36	18	—	17	17	20	17
Post 1989	61	100	64	82	100	83	83	80	83
N	49	3	52	359	31	390	223	12	235

Table 5.2 shows that the majority (over four out of five) of equal opportunities school policies were developed after the ERA; in contrast with three out of five English and Welsh LEA

policies. In the Welsh survey, all the primary schools which had developed an equal opportunities policy had done so after the ERA and in some cases as late as 1992.

The LEA responses in the project survey do not concur with the findings of the EOC (1988), suggesting that perhaps those responsible for equal opportunities in local authorities today may have limited knowledge of earlier policy developments - this was a factor noted in the case study LEAs.

The impetus for an equal opportunities policy

Schools and LEAs in the survey were asked where the impetus for introducing an equal opportunities policy on gender had come from. Of importance here was the accuracy of recall of the respondent, the origins of LEA policy development and whether local education authorities were perceived as having played a role in generating equal opportunities policy initiatives. Table 5.3 describes LEA and school responses to a list of potentially influential groups and policies.

According to the LEAs (for both England and Wales), the original impetus for equal opportunities policies was perceived as coming from a variety of sources, but in particular 70 per cent of respondents named in-house LEA officers. Thirty five per cent of English LEA respondents identified a group of interested teachers, 25 per cent named TVEI, and headteachers and Teacher Unions were identified as influential by approximately 20 per cent.

Table 5.3 also illustrates the pattern of response from English and Welsh primary and secondary schools. Approximately half the primary school respondents in England and Wales perceived the LEA as having provided an impetus for the original equal opportunities policy, even though many of these policies were only recently introduced.

Headteachers, to a much greater extent than teachers, were viewed as playing an important part in these developments (being referred to by 44 per cent and 17 per cent of English and Welsh primary school respondents respectively). Given the relatively recent nature of these policies it is not surprising that groups of school governors, and the inclusion of equal opportunities in the OFSTED criteria were mentioned by only a minority (approximately 18 per cent of respondents).

LEA influences were referred to by a smaller proportion of secondary school respondents in England (37 per cent compared with 51 per cent of English primary schools). However, eight out of the 12 Welsh secondary schools in the survey reported the influence of LEAs in encouraging equal opportunities development. Other identified influences on secondary schools included committed teachers, headteachers and the introduction of TVEI in secondary schools (a view that was corroborated by the school case studies; see Chapter 6).

Table 5.3   Impetus for the introduction of equal opportunities [1]

per cent

	LEAs			Primary Schools			Secondary Schools		
	E	W	E&W	E	W	E&W	E	W	E&W
LEA	n/a	n/a	n/a	51	48	51	37	67	39
Group of LEA Officers	69	67	69	n/a	n/a	n/a	n/a	n/a	3
Group of Governors	2	—	2	18	19	18	17	18	17
Parent Governors	n/a	n/a	n/a	3	—	3	3	—	3
Group of Interested Parents	—	—	—	1	—	1	4	—	3
Group of Headteachers	22	33	23	45	39	44	47	42	47
Group of Interested Teachers	35	—	33	18	3	17	50	42	50
Teacher Unions	18	33	19	8	—	7	5	—	5
National Curriculum	10	33	12	10	13	10	7	25	8
TVEI	25	33	25	n/a	n/a	n/a	38	17	37
OFSTED Criteria	2	33	4	17	19	17	9	8	9
Careers Service	8	—	8	n/a	n/a	n/a	3	—	3
Children's Act	4	33	6	5	—	5	4	17	5
Others [2]	28	67	50	7	3	20	12	—	20
N	49	3	52	359	31	390	223	12	235

[1]   Respondents were asked to indicate all factors that applied

[2]   E.g. senior management, reorganisation of school

The National Curriculum does not appear to have been a key impetus in equal opportunities policy-making, nor indeed does the introduction of parent governors (a point returned to later).

Teacher unions appear to have played some part in LEA equal opportunity policy initiatives but had little reported impetus in primary or secondary schools. LEA influences on school equal opportunities policy were reported as having been relatively strong, particularly in primary schools, followed closely by headteachers. Influences inside the schools (such as teachers, headteachers and TVEI curriculum developments) were viewed as playing a more important role in secondary schools. CTCs reported that their main influences in this area have come from executive management teams. Given their recent creation and independent status, they would be unlikely to have been influenced by LEAs.

The coverage of equal opportunities policies

LEAs and schools were asked to indicate (using a given list) to whom equal opportunity policies applied. Table 5.4 illustrates the range of applications of current equal opportunities policies. Approximately one-fifth of primary schools were unable to answer the question as they reported not having a policy - though some of them reported being in the process of policy development.

Table 5.4   Applicability of equal opportunities policy [1]

per cent

	LEAs			Primary Schools			Secondary Schools		
	E	W	E&W	E	W	E&W	E	W	E&W
Pupils	74	33	72	77	68	76	93	83	92
Teachers	92	100	92	74	55	73	91	83	90
Support Staff	84	100	85	69	45	67	83	75	83
Care Staff	74	67	73	36	29	35	45	25	44
Parents	41	—	39	40	19	38	35	8	33
LEA Officers	92	67	90	n/a	n/a	n/a	n/a	n/a	n/a
Governors/Other	4	—	3	2	—	1	1	—	2
No Such Policy	2	—	2	19	26	19	4	8	4
N	49	3	52	359	31	390	223	12	235

[1]   Respondents were asked to indicate more than one where applicable

English LEA respondents indicated that between 80 per cent and 90 per cent of current policies covered LEA officers, teachers and support staff. The emphasis on employment issues might account for the fact that only 72 per cent of LEA equal opportunities policies included pupils.

Parents and school governors as yet appear not to be included to any great extent in such policy initiatives, in particular in Welsh LEAs.

Primary school respondents reported that in most cases policies tended to include pupils, teachers and support staff. Equal opportunities policies, however, were less likely to cover care staff and parents, and only two per cent of English primary school policies applied to parent governors.

The pattern amongst secondary schools was slightly different. Equal opportunities policies here appeared to apply equally to teaching staff and pupils, perhaps because the emphasis on employment may be stronger here than in primary schools. The CTCs also reflected this emphasis, with rather more respondents reporting that equal opportunities policies referred to teachers and parents rather than pupils.

Implementation of the equal opportunities policy

Of considerable importance to the effectiveness of equal opportunities policies is the method of implementation and the commitment of the school to promoting gender equality. School respondents were asked whether their institutions had established any specialist structures to develop equal opportunities (listed below in Table 5.5). They were also asked to identify their school's specific involvement in equal opportunities, thus adding further insight into the current structuring of equal opportunities responsibilities in schools today.

The strategies which seem currently to have been adopted by primary schools are diverse, with no one strategy commonly found. Specialist working groups on equal opportunities (whether general or specific) appear to be rare (17 per cent). One-fifth of primary school respondents reported having teachers with special responsibility for gender issues, though only two per cent had a specialist coordinator for gender in the school. Not surprisingly, therefore, such respondents (for the purposes of the questionnaire) were more likely to have been headteachers or deputy headteachers with overall responsibility for school development. Significantly, most claimed to have 'an interest in equal opportunities' (49 per cent for the English and 67 per cent of the Welsh primary school respondents), rather than a special responsibility, with five per cent claiming no involvement in equal opportunities.

In contrast, a relatively higher proportion of secondary schools reported having established working groups (57 per cent) or having coordinators (33 per cent) for equal opportunities. A small number of secondary schools reported appointing teachers with special responsibility for gender and the same number had specialist working groups or coordinators on gender issues (six per cent in both cases). Interestingly, the CTCs revealed a higher proportion (56 per cent) with working groups on equal opportunities, or with a vice principal designated as having special responsibility for equal opportunities.

Questionnaire respondents from English secondary schools were unlikely to be equal opportunity coordinators. Over half were officers or managers with an interest in equal opportunities, with only 40 per cent claiming to have a special responsibility for gender. Given the small proportion of working groups on gender, the respondents were unlikely to be members of such a group. Half of the English male respondents, in fact, were headteachers (compared with only 25 per cent of female respondents) and well over half the respondents from Welsh secondary schools were part of senior management (50 per cent headteachers, 25 per cent deputy heads or 13 per cent heads of upper school). Similarly, CTC respondents, who were largely Principals (44 per cent) and Vice-Principals (33 per cent), claimed to have an interest rather than a responsibility for gender issues (see Table 5.6 below).

Table 5.5   The organisation of responsibility for equal opportunities (gender) in schools

per cent

	Primary Schools			Secondary Schools		
	E	W	E&W	E	W	E&W
Working Group on Equal Opportunities (General)	14	13	14	58	50	57
Working Group on Equal Opportunities (Gender)	2	7	3	6	8	6
Other Working Group [1]	6	—	6	13	8	10
Teacher with Special Responsibility	22	19	22	38	33	38
Coordinator for Equal Opportunities (General)	12	10	12	33	25	33
Coordinator for Equal Opportunities (Gender)	2	3	2	6	—	6
Governor; Vice Principal	2	—	2	—	—	—
Other Individual	11	—	8	7	—	7
N	359	31	390	223	12	235

[1]   E.g. special needs, multicultural, race equality

LEA respondents revealed through their job titles the diversity of roles which currently incorporate equal opportunities responsibilities. Although 51 per cent of respondents identified themselves as having special responsibility for gender issues, they were to be found working under more than 37 different job titles. Only three job titles contained the term 'equal opportunities' (such as inspector or education officer for equal opportunities).

This range of titles bears witness to the impact of the organisational changes that have occurred during the last 10 years. Case study data reveal substantial staff reductions in LEAs, which may remove or substantially change the responsibilities of the specialist equal opportunities officer or advisor. Many of those with continuing responsibility for the area are working with fragmented or multiple job descriptions, (e.g. enterprise activities, cross curricular concerns), and thus are less likely to be identified specifically as equal opportunities specialists. Some commented on the difficulty this represents to the public when trying to contact individuals with designated responsibilities.

Table 5.6   **Respondents' involvement in equal opportunities (gender) issues in the LEA/school**

per cent

	LEAs			Primary Schools			Secondary Schools		
	E	W	E&W	E	W	E&W	E	W	E&W
Special Responsibility	57	33	**55**	23	13	**20**	43	55	**53**
Officer/manager with interest	35	67	**37**	57	67	**58**	49	38	**49**
Member of working group	4	—	**4**	3	3	**3**	6	—	**6**
Not involved	2	—	**2**	5	7	**5**	1	9	**1**
N	49	3	52	359	31	390	223	12	235

Such extensive turnover and reorganisation of LEA staff has considerable implications for their length and depth of experience of equal opportunities issues. Two-thirds of the LEA respondents reported that their post had been created within the last five years (a quarter occupied posts created before 1988). Nevertheless, the majority of LEA respondents saw themselves as having some responsibility for equal opportunities, with only two per cent reporting that they were not involved at all with such issues.

The commitment of schools and LEAs to equal opportunities issues

The impetus for developing equal opportunities policies in LEAs and schools currently appears to rest with a range of individuals. In LEAs most of the development work seems to be the responsibility of LEA officers and equal opportunities advisors and, to a lesser extent, the Chief Education Officer/Director. Fewer headteachers, teachers or TVEI coordinators appear to have been responsible for initiating changes in LEA policies, (see Table 5.7 below).

In approximately 50 per cent of primary schools, the responsibility for initiating changes to the equal opportunities policy came from the headteacher or deputy head. A similar pattern was found in secondary schools, with responsibility for initiating changes in equal opportunities viewed as equally split between the individual headteacher (34 per cent) and a group of teachers (36 per cent).

Table 5.7   **Responsibility for initiating changes in equal opportunities policies** [1]

per cent

	LEAs			Primary Schools			Secondary Schools		
	E	W	E&W	E	W	E&W	E	W	E&W
CEO/Director	31	67	33	—	—	—	—	—	—
Senior Managers	10	—	10	n/a	n/a	n/a	n/a	n/a	n/a
LEA Officers	43	33	42	n/a	n/a	n/a	n/a	n/a	n/a
Group of Headteachers	6	—	6	n/a	n/a	n/a	n/a	n/a	n/a
EO Officer/Advisor	39	67	40	n/a	n/a	n/a	12	—	11
Individual Headteacher	n/a	n/a	n/a	43	32	42	33	50	34
Deputy Head (Curriculum)	n/a	n/a	n/a	n/a	n/a	n/a	27	17	26
Deputy Head (Pastoral)	n/a	n/a	n/a	12	3	11	18	25	19
TVEI Coordinator	n/a	n/a	n/a	n/a	n/a	n/a	19	17	19
Teacher Special Responsibility	n/a	n/a	n/a	8	3	8	27	33	27
Group of Teachers	n/a	n/a	n/a	14	7	14	36	33	36
Other	28	33	26	12	6	11	10	8	11
N	49	3	52	359	31	390	223	12	235

[1]   Respondents were requested to indicate more than one factor where appropriate

A major factor in the successful development and implementation of equal opportunities policies in schools is the commitment of schools and LEAs (see Table 5.8). Yet, schools and LEAs were not described by the respondents as giving gender a high priority. At best, 42 per cent of primary school respondents in England and Wales chose, instead, to describe their school stance on gender equality as an 'integral part' of the school. This is similar in tone to the 'equal entitlement' approach in which children are reported as all being treated alike.

Table 5.8   **Current stances on gender equality** [1]

per cent

	LEAs			Primary Schools			Secondary Schools		
	E	W	E&W	E	W	E&W	E	W	E&W
One of Number	18	—	18	23	23	23	28	17	28
Actively Developing	31	—	31	14	3	13	22	25	22
Moderate Interest	29	33	31	9	20	10	11	8	11
Integral Part	8	33	10	42	33	42	28	17	28
High Priority	4	33	6	5	10	6	8	—	8
Just Started	2	—	2	6	7	6	2	8	2
Not on the Agenda	—	—	—	1	3	1	—	8	1
Not Interested	—	—	—	—	—	—	1	—	1
No Response	8	—	2	—	—	—	—	17	—
N	49	3	52	359	31	390	223	12	235

[1]   Respondents were requested to make only one response

In contrast, just under 30 per cent of secondary schools described gender equality as integral to their work. Gender issues in 28 per cent of secondary schools were described as 'one of a number' of issues being tackled at present; whilst 20 per cent of secondary schools (in comparison with 13 per cent of primary schools) were reported to be 'actively developing an interest' in gender.

LEAs appeared to be more actively developing gender equality or to have a moderate interest in the subject; though rather than giving it high priority, it tended to be viewed as integral to the authority's work.

Over half the CTCs (57 per cent) in the survey reported actively developing equal opportunities policies and for the rest, gender issues were one of a number of concerns. Significantly, 22 per cent of CTCs were reported as giving the issue high priority, compared with 8 per cent of secondary schools.

5.3   LEA INFLUENCE ON SCHOOL POLICY AND PRACTICE

LEA approaches to changing school practice tended to be diverse in the past and there is clear evidence from the case studies that there is little standardisation of approach as a result of the reforms. The different histories of equal opportunities policy-making, special local contexts and the impact of the reforms on the funding and administration of schools have affected the ways in which LEAs currently influence, or choose to perceive their influence, on schools.

For example, educational reforms have significantly affected staffing patterns within LEAs, in some cases with major restructuring and redundancies, affecting the ways in which LEAs make contact and choose to support schools. A consequence of such reorganisation within English (and now Welsh LEAs, who were also undergoing restructuring into unitary authorities at the time of the research) is the forgotten history of past strategies for providing support to schools. In at least two of the case study LEAs, there had been a history of commitment and activism around equal opportunities involving both the authority and the schools. Data from these studies suggest that few if any records of past equal opportunities initiatives, or their evaluation, are readily available. Retrieving past policy statements and reports tended to be serendipitous and erratic. Many of the 'activists' were reported to have now left public service and their initiatives (e.g. in-service education or training for school staff (INSET) provision, resource centres or school networks), which had generally been small-scale and short-lived, are now perceived as part of LEA history.

Some case study schools commended (sometimes nostalgically) LEA equal opportunities advisors and their work. However, such commendation and information was not always available to current LEA officers. In certain cases the OFSTED inspector, if previously an equal opportunities advisor, had a clearer memory of school-focused initiatives than current LEA staff.

The impact of the reforms on LEA - school relations in terms of marginalising LEA influence was expressed in various ways in the survey. A minority of English and Welsh LEA respondents, for example, reported being involved in the introduction of the National Curriculum and other curricular and assessment reforms (such as TVEI, GCSE and GNVQs). As few as 12 per cent of LEA respondents reported helping with support and training, and 22 per cent reported helping with curriculum development and guidelines, and INSET for the National Curriculum. Again, a small minority of respondents recognised the potential of the National Curriculum to improve gender equality in schools, for example by increasing entitlement, raising teacher awareness and providing facilities (10-12 per cent). Interestingly, however, only eight per cent saw the reforms as detracting from equal opportunities.

Fewer than a fifth of LEA respondents reported helping introduce GCSE (through subject support, INSET/advisory support), TVEI (through coordinating curriculum development) and GNVQ (through information sharing, guidance and training). The majority of LEAs did not appear to have an active involvement in the reforms affecting schools.

Similarly, LEA respondents did not identify many ways in which the LEA was currently influencing gender equality in primary or secondary schools. When asked, through open ended questions, to indicate the range of strategies currently being used, between 20 per cent and 30 per cent referred to LEA influence on primary schools through policies and policy statements, INSET and advisory support, and preparation for OFSTED inspections. Table 5.9 shows that English LEA respondents believed that their influence on gender issues in primary schools appeared to have increased (in nearly half the English cases and 67 per cent in Wales), whilst, in contrast, a third thought that LEA influence had become more limited.

LEAs were asked to evaluate their current influence on school practice in terms of gender equality. A minority - between 30 per cent and 40 per cent - reported influencing schools through policy statements or through advisory support and/or help. Similarly, a minority considered that they had a continuing influence through INSET and policies, such as TVEI, in secondary schools. When asked to compare LEA influence in 1994 with that of a decade earlier, almost half of the LEAs claimed that they currently had more influence on both primary and secondary schools. However, a third of the LEAs in England (but no Welsh LEAs) claimed that their influence was more limited at primary level (see Table 5.9).

LEA involvement in secondary school gender equality initiatives appeared slightly stronger, with a similar level (46 per cent) of English respondents reporting more influence currently (and 33 per cent of Welsh LEAs). A slightly higher proportion of LEAs in the survey reported a reduced influence on equal opportunities work in secondary schools when compared with primary schools. LEA involvement in advisory work related to TVEI, INSET and inspection (40 per cent) was felt to be more important than that focusing on policy development.

Most LEA respondents referred to the LEA role in offering advice to schools rather than in determining particular policies and practices. For some, such support and advice is an extension of prior involvement; for others, it represents a reduction of commitment; and for yet others, it is a new venture. The case studies showed the extent to which the advice and support provided varied in depth and range among the LEAs. Such variety could be accounted for in terms of commitment to the issue of equal opportunities and this depended considerably on the policy approach adopted by the LEA. It is suggested that there were three identifiable LEA stances towards equal opportunities: interventionist, entrepreneurial and laissez-faire.

Table 5.9   **LEA view of their influence on schools in terms of gender equality**

			per cent	
LEA		E	W	E&W
Primary	*LEA influence on school (1984-1994)*			
	More limited now	30	—	30
	More influence now	48	67	50
Secondary	*LEA Influence on school (1984-1994)*			
	More limited now	38	33	38
	More influence now	46	33	48
N		49	3	52

● Where LEAs have developed a highly *interventionist* strategy, equal opportunities appeared to be well coordinated from the centre and involved schools 'buying in' to an agreed programme as part of the renegotiated school - LEA partnership.

● Where LEAs have been *entrepreneurial,* they have obtained equal opportunities funds (e.g. through TVEI and Department of Employment (ED) initiatives on careers education) to be used as part of the service delivery. In this case, school autonomy in policy development is promoted and LEA support offered for focused and often transitory initiatives, dependent as they are on short term government grants.

● LEAs with *laissez faire* approaches promote school autonomy. Here, deliberate promotion of equal opportunities by the LEA would be seen as unnecessarily interventionist. The LEA expects each school to define its own agenda. Advisory support to schools, in this case, is seen as market-led and minimal; in practice, it appears to be integrated within broader concerns about curriculum planning, school development and/or value-added (VA) strategies.

When asked to indicate the extent to which LEAs were providing services to support or advise them on equal opportunities issues, schools in fact did not report high levels of provision.

Surveyed primary schools in England and Wales identified INSET provision (31 per cent) as the most significant form of LEA service. Smaller numbers of schools indicated that they received help via resource centres, advisory teachers, the local inspectorate or an identified equal opportunities officer. As few as two per cent of English, and no Welsh, primary, schools reported receiving financial support for the promotion of equal opportunities.

Table 5.10   LEA support and/or advice on equal opportunities [1]

per cent

Type of LEA Service	Primary Schools			Secondary Schools		
	E	W	E&W	E	W	E&W
Resource Centre	12	7	12	16	8	16
Subject/Advisory Teacher	16	13	16	31	25	31
The Local Inspectorate	16	3	15	19	8	19
Equal Opportunities Officer	12	7	12	15	17	15
Coordinated School Network	4	—	4	8	—	8
INSET Provision	31	32	31	44	50	43
Financial Support	2	—	2	7	8	7
Careers Service	n/a	n/a	n/a	11	17	11
TVEI	n/a	n/a	n/a	8	—	8
Other	10	6	12	9	—	5
N	359	31	390	223	12	235

[1]   Respondents were asked to indicate more than one form of service where appropriate

In contrast, support from LEAs to secondary schools for equal opportunities seemed to be received not only in the form of INSET (40-50 per cent), but also in the guise of subject/advisory teachers (31 per cent). Seven per cent, a higher percentage than for primary schools, reported receiving financial assistance for equal opportunities work. Less than a fifth of primary and secondary schools reported that help had come via resource centres, the local inspectorate, or identified equal opportunities officers; and fewer than eight per cent were working within a coordinated school network.

The case studies additionally identified, in some schools, a sense of isolation and the consequent lack of sharing of experiences between schools and LEAs in the post-reform period. Evidence here suggests that one of the least positive outcomes of LMS has been the lack of local, well-planned and coherent INSET for equal opportunities, with a resultant loss of shared expertise and practices. Some headteachers (especially from selective grant-maintained schools) appeared actively to be seeking ways to share their understanding and strategies for improving pupil performance, although it is not clear to what extent they prioritised gender issues. Meanwhile, others continued to look to the LEA to coordinate school networks over and above the designated climate of competition among schools.

It is difficult to know from the data available to what extent the support and advice claimed to have been given by LEAs to schools was received, and whether it was equally available to all schools in an authority or only available to those which responded positively to such provision What is of significance, however, is the relatively low level of support reported to have been received by schools, compared with the more positive picture concerning LEA influence provided by the LEAs themselves.

LEA monitoring and training for equal opportunities

A key role which remains the responsibility of LEAs is in the monitoring of school performance (especially 16+ and 18+ examination performance). Schools are required to provide relevant information to LEAs, resulting in publication of the performance of each school by the DfE. LEAs are also mandated to collect information on pupil performance by gender. If they so wish, they can also collect similar statistics on teaching and other school staff.

Emphasis upon patterns of achievement and the publication of examination results appears to have encouraged (particularly at school level) greater interest in emergent gendered patterns of achievement. Thus, LEAs and schools have started to publish detailed gender breakdowns of patterns of examination performance. Additionally, schools are also being asked to provide gender breakdowns for SATs and others are voluntarily sending their 'raw' GCSE scores to the A-Level Information System (ALIS) and other projects promising assistance in providing a 'value-added' approach to pupil performance.

The responsibility for monitoring performance by gender and the provision of training opportunities and advice, especially in relation to improving performance, has to some extent shifted from LEAs to schools. With the introduction of Grants for Educational Support and Training (GEST), which has relocated in-service training budgets to schools, and LMS, which has given schools budgetary control, the pattern of INSET provision for equal opportunities has changed substantially. Some LEAs have been compelled substantially to reduce equal opportunities provision due to the loss of advisory staff and identified equal opportunities posts. This has led to concern being expressed by some schools and advisors about the ability of LEAs to achieve authority-wide monitoring and INSET on equal opportunities as a result of the reforms - although for some authorities, this had never been a goal in the first place.

Table 5.11   **LEA service before the introduction of LMS** [1]

per cent

	Type of LEA Service	E	W	E&W
Monitoring	Monitoring gender equality for teachers	18	—	17
	Monitoring gender equality for pupils	16	33	18
	Monitoring male and female pupils' performance	18	33	19
Training	Providing equal opportunities training for governors	37	33	36
	Providing equal opportunities training for senior managers	18	33	19
	Providing equal opportunities training for classroom teachers	20	33	21
Advisory	Providing advice on gender aspects of careers education	27	33	29
	Coordinating TVEI	32	33	32
N		49	3	52

[1]   LEA respondents were asked to indicate all that applied

LMS, in fact, appears not to have been evenly introduced, with almost half the LEAs surveyed claiming to have introduced it into primary schools in 1990, yet only a quarter of the primary schools claimed that LMS had been introduced by that year and 50 per cent reported its introduction one or two years later. Similar discrepancies were found with the secondary school population.

When asked for information about the pattern of monitoring and training services offered to schools prior to the introduction of LMS, the response was more muted than might have been expected. Approximately one-fifth of LEA respondents reported offering support for monitoring gender differences amongst teachers or pupils and providing training for equal opportunities. Such responses may, however, refer to the years immediately prior to the introduction of LMS when services might already have been run down as a result of anticipated reductions in LEA staff.

In contrast, the services reported by LEAs as currently being provided by them (post-LMS) appear to be considerable. Table 5.12 indicates that nearly all LEAs (90 per cent) claim to be monitoring gender performance of pupils, and eight out of ten claim to be providing equal opportunities training for governors and classroom teachers. The extent to which they are doing this, however, is variable. Clearly, one would need to investigate whether this provision involves offering one course or many, whether it is taken up, and, if so, in what numbers. What the data suggest, however, is the relative importance of such equal opportunities strategies for LEAs in the post-reform context.

Although the number of Welsh LEAs in the project survey is small, the figures suggest that some differences exist between England and Wales in relation to the monitoring of teachers, and opportunities for equal opportunities training for schools (as opposed to senior managers and governors).

Schools were asked to report on the whether they had actually received such monitoring or training services from LEAs. Clearly the proportions responding positively were lower than those reported by the LEAs. Of note - see Table 5.13 - is that monitoring services or feedback appear to have been received by less than a third of secondary schools in England (a half in Wales), and that less than one-fifth of primary schools reported benefitting from such services - a pattern perhaps attributable to the emphasis upon examination achievement at 16+ and 18+.

Table 5.12   LEA services currently being provided for schools [1]

per cent

	Type of LEA Service	E	W	E&W
Monitoring	Monitoring gender equality for teachers	53	33	52
	Monitoring gender equality for pupils	39	67	40
	Monitoring male and female pupils' performance	92	67	90
Training	Providing equal opportunities training for governors	86	67	85
	Providing equal opportunities training for senior managers	76	100	77
	Providing equal opportunities training for classroom teachers	84	33	81
Advisory	Providing advice on gender aspects of careers education	69	33	67
	Coordinating TVEI	59	33	58
N		49	3	52

[1]   LEA respondents were asked to indicate all that applied

The main form of support for schools appears to have been equal opportunities training for governors (45 per cent of primary and 37 per cent of secondary schools). Approximately 70 per cent of primary and secondary schools respondents did not report receiving equal opportunities training for senior managers, class teachers and careers advisors (the latter for secondary only).

Thus although the majority of LEA respondents claimed they are making provision for school equal opportunities monitoring and training, the proportions appear to be far higher than responses from schools would suggest. The move towards 'service delivery' models reported in the case studies may account for the limited opportunities and lack of incentive in terms of take-up.

If schools are failing to report having had LEA support for equal opportunities, for whatever reason, a key concern is whether LMS has encouraged school governing bodies to assume some of these vacated responsibilities. However, Table 5.14 indicates that only a third of governing bodies are reported to be monitoring gender performance in secondary schools (fewer in Wales)

91

and fewer yet (11 per cent and three per cent) of primary schools are doing the same. Equal opportunities training seems to have been targeted towards governors (21 per cent) rather than towards senior managers and teachers (fewer than 12 per cent).

Table 5.13   **Monitoring and training services received from LEAs by primary and secondary schools[1]**

per cent

		Primary Schools			Secondary Schools		
		E	W	E&W	E	W	E&W
Monitoring	Monitoring gender equality for teachers	17	3	16	19	17	19
	Monitoring gender equality for pupils	14	3	13	15	8	15
	Monitoring male and female pupils' performance	18	13	18	28	50	29
Training	Providing equal opportunities training for governors	45	45	45	39	17	37
	Providing equal opportunities training for senior managers	36	23	35	29	25	30
	Providing equal opportunities training for classroom teachers	30	23	30	37	33	37
Advisory	Providing advice on gender aspects of careers education	n/a	n/a	n/a	33	25	32
	Coordinating TVEI	n/a	n/a	n/a	71	75	71
N		359	31	390	223	12	235

[1]   School respondents were asked to indicate all that applied

LMS does not seem to have encouraged the majority of school governing bodies to monitor staffing structure, pupil organisation or performance, nor to offer training in equal opportunities.

Data from the CTC sub-sample suggest that similar patterns are reflected in CTC governing bodies, 22 per cent of these are reported as having taken responsibility for monitoring equal opportunities among staff and among pupils. However, only one CTC governing body claimed to have taken responsibility for monitoring pupil performance, and for equal opportunities training.

Table 5.14   Responsibilities undertaken by the governing bodies of primary and secondary schools, since LMS [1]

per cent

		Primary Schools			Secondary Schools		
		E	W	E&W	E	W	E&W
Monitoring	Monitoring gender equality for teachers	20	13	20	23	17	23
	Monitoring gender equality for pupils	19	19	19	21	17	21
	Monitoring male and female pupils' performance	11	3	11	33	25	33
Training	Providing equal opportunities training for governors	22	13	21	19	8	17
	Providing equal opportunities training for senior managers	10	3	9	9	—	9
	Providing equal opportunities training for classroom teachers	12	7	12	11	—	9
Advisory	Providing advice on gender aspects of careers education	n/a	n/a	n/a	6	8	6
	Coordinating TVEI	n/a	n/a	n/a	9	—	9
N		359	31	390	223	12	235

[1]   School respondents were asked to indicate all that applied

5.4   THE NEW INSPECTORATE (OFSTED)

In 1993 the new inspectorate (OFSTED) was set up, taking on some of the powers of the HMI (later disbanded). The new inspectors' work in specially constructed teams of trained individuals with varied experience, which are compelled to bid for the right to inspect primary, secondary and special schools. In 1993, equal opportunities was included as one of the criteria for school inspections, and thus included as an item, in each published inspection report.

Amplification of the evaluation criteria for equal opportunities in English schools was described in the *Handbook for the Inspection of Schools* (OFSTED 1993b, p. 56) as follows:

> *The school has a clear policy which it monitors. Teachers appreciate how factors such as ethnicity, bilingualism, gender, social circumstances and giftedness may affect learning; they know how to plan work, and organise and manage classes to take into account of the different needs of pupils, while maintaining consistently high expectations. Where practice is good all pupils have planned access to a broad and balanced curriculum. Their access is not merely formal but functional so that all may achieve good standards and develop their talents to the full.*

Factors identified by OFSTED which were to be considered when reviewing evidence for the inspection included achievement of different groups of pupils, school policy, curricular access and content, monitoring of examination and test results, admissions policies, staffing and staff development, learning resources and accommodation. Significantly inspectors were required to be aware of the relevant recent legislation and also the Sex Discrimination Act (1975) and the Race Relations Act (1976).

As is evident from the above extract, gender was one of a number of elements included under the umbrella term of equal opportunities. The OFSTED criteria as above were still in place during the time of the research and were those referred to by schools and LEAs in the survey and case studies, though the criteria were subsequently revised and interpreted more broadly in later inspection framework documents.

For Wales, equal opportunities was included as a 'Technical Paper' in the Welsh *Framework for the Inspection of Schools* (OHMCI 1993). This covered much the same ground as that of the English document, though it appeared slightly more proactive in referring additionally to teaching about equal opportunities.

> *Such teaching is likely to occur in a wide range of contexts in the majority of schools. Important issues for consideration will include the extent to which the*

school seeks to ensure that pupils are presented with a balanced range of evidence when controversial issues are dealt with.
(p. 51)

At the time of the research, only a relatively small proportion of survey schools had experienced the new mode of inspection and were able to assess its impact on the promotion and development of equal opportunities. Twenty-three primary schools and 58 secondary schools in the sample had been inspected (and none of the CTCs).

According to LEAs, which were in some instances carefully assessing OFSTED reports on equal opportunities (see also Chapter 6), OFSTED inspections were seen as having a positive influence on equal opportunities. Over two-thirds of LEAs in England and Wales reported that OFSTED inspections had raised the profile of equal opportunities, and a further 60 per cent suggested that such inspections had also encouraged a higher general interest in schools. Only a small minority (four to six per cent) reacted negatively to OFSTED's role in relation to equal opportunities, seeing it either as irrelevant or as providing a disincentive for action.

Table 5.15   **Impact of OFSTED inspections on equal opportunities work in schools** [1]

per cent

	E	W	E&W
Encouraged a general interest in equal opportunities	61	67	62
Raised the profile of equal opportunities	69	100	71
Provided a strong incentive for equal opportunities	35	67	37
Were irrelevant to equal opportunities	6	—	6
Provided a disincentive to equal opportunities	4	—	4
N	49	3	52

[1]   LEA respondents were asked to indicate all factors that applied

This confidence in the impact of OFSTED on promoting gender issues was, in some cases, supported by LEA staff. Case study notes suggest that some LEAs currently offer considerable support to schools in advance of an inspection by providing manuals, checklists to help prepare answers for the inspectors' questions, and advice on the sort of material that needs to be collected prior to a visit (see Chapter 6). Such support has clearly helped signal the importance of equal opportunities, highlighting the need to satisfy the inspectors on this issue.

Yet, the kinds of information actually requested by OFSTED, as reported by those schools which had been inspected, were perhaps not as comprehensive nor as detailed as might be expected. For example, a female Deputy Head of a mixed comprehensive, with a well established and confident tradition of working on equal opportunities in the school, had mixed feelings about the quality of the inspectors' conclusions on equal opportunities:

> *I think the things that have disappointed me in terms of OFSTED is that it was good to see it [the equal opportunities criteria] there and we felt quite positive about that in our framework. We've used that with staff and it has been useful. We've really got to tackle this and this is an important part, but actually having read reports of schools I know well, who have OFSTED reports on equal opportunities, and actually nothing much is happening, I found [that] very disappointing. Two schools I know pretty well came out well in terms of equal opportunities issues and we don't believe it - but it's nice to see it written down in the framework. There hasn't been very much comment in OFSTED reports I've read about management patterns and the lack of senior women and yet there is a lot of consideration of management and how the school is being run and so on.*
>
> (Case study notes)

Table 5.16 indicates that, when inspected, nearly all schools were asked for their equal opportunities policy statement. Significantly, the information most frequently requested by inspectors on equal opportunities included:

- evidence of the existence of school policy - 93 per cent and 78 per cent respectively for English primary and secondary schools;

- curriculum access - 73 per cent and 53 per cent respectively for English primary and secondary schools;

- equal opportunities as a cross-curricular dimension - 67 per cent and 60 per cent respectively for English primary and secondary schools;

- pupil achievement - 60 per cent and 67 per cent respectively for English primary and secondary schools; and

- class management and teaching - 60 per cent and 38 per cent respectively for English primary and secondary schools.

Table 5.16   Equal opportunities information requested from primary and secondary schools prior to inspection by OFSTED

per cent

	Primary Schools			Secondary Schools		
	E	W	E&W	E	W	E&W
School policy statements	93	—	82	78	33	75
Male/Female staff pattern	47	—	41	43	100	46
EO as cross curricular dimension	67	50	65	60	—	57
Admissions policies	27	—	24	16	—	15
Pupil intake patterns	20	—	18	19	—	18
Pupil grouping arrangement	53	—	47	50	67	51
Pupil achievement	60	—	53	67	100	69
Curriculum access	73	50	71	53	33	52
Curriculum content	40	—	35	34	33	34
Class management and teaching	60	—	53	38	—	36
Library resources	33	—	29	16	—	15
Sexual harassment	—	—	—	14	—	13
Pastoral provision	40	50	41	31	33	31
Use of support teachers	20	—	18	17	—	16
N	15	2	17	58	3	61

The two Welsh primary schools which had been inspected reported very little interest in equal opportunities, though interest appeared more marked in the three Welsh secondary schools which had been inspected, in particular, concerning pupil achievement and staffing patterns.

Of particular note is how few inspectors asked about aspects of the hidden curriculum (see Chapter 2), such as sexual harassment, which can affect pupil achievement; library resources, which are particularly important for the development of reading skills; and pastoral provision, which, for example, includes sex education.

Teachers in case study schools were rather more ambivalent about the role of OFSTED inspections and how they had promoted equal opportunities. For some it was a question of facilitating the promotion of equal opportunities by compelling inspectors to ask a range of relevant questions. For others, there was disbelief at some of the published reports, especially

97

those which were seen as far too complimentary where practice did not appear to match the inspectors' descriptions. Clearly much depended upon the awareness, skill and interest of each inspector in addressing equal opportunities and gender issues. See Chapter 6 where school perceptions of OFSTED are discussed more fully.

It is important, however, to note the significance attached by schools and LEAs to the possibilities contained within the OFSTED framework. For example, the new inspectorate appears to provide a mechanism by which equal opportunities practice in schools can be monitored more effectively.

5.5   CONCLUSIONS

Equal opportunities policy making

- Two-thirds of English and Welsh LEAs reported having specific policies on gender and three-quarters had both a specific policy on gender and an equal opportunities policy which included gender.

- The majority of schools reported having equal opportunities policies covering gender, with a substantial group of Welsh primary and secondary schools being in the process of developing such policies.

- 80 per cent of school policies on equal opportunities were developed after 1989.

- The main impetus for first introducing equal opportunities policies in LEAs came from officers and teachers. Officers are now solely responsible for developing LEA policies.

- The main impetus for introducing equal opportunities in primary schools came from LEAs and headteachers, and in secondary schools from LEAs, headteachers, teachers and TVEI. The development of such policies is now mainly the responsibility of the schools themselves, with parents and parent governors currently appearing not to be playing any major role.

- LEA equal opportunities policies appear to provide greater coverage on employment issues than on pupil performance.

- Parents, care staff and parent governors tend not to be included within school equal opportunities policies.

- Fewer primary than secondary schools had equal opportunities policies in place, and primary schools tended to develop them at a later date. One of the main reasons for this is that primary staff tend to see equal opportunities as integral to their practice rather than as a discrete priority.

- Over 50 per cent of secondary schools reported having working groups or coordinators for equal opportunities, some having teachers with specific equal opportunities responsibilities. Less evident is a coordinating role specifically for gender. Over 50 per cent of CTCs reported having teachers with special responsibilities for gender.

- Gender equality was not reported as a high priority in secondary schools; the most common description was that there were several related issues being tackled or being actively developed. Over a half of CTCs reported actively developing gender policies, whilst a further fifth claimed to have given equal opportunities a high priority.

- Equal opportunities responsibilities in LEAs appear to be disparate, with few specified posts for gender and staff with such responsibilities having diverse job descriptions. For the LEAs surveyed, commitment to equal opportunities tended to be described as 'moderate' or 'actively developing an interest' rather than as a high priority or integral to all work.

LEA influence on equal opportunities in schools

- LEAs reported low levels of involvement in introducing curriculum reforms in schools and in influencing primary and secondary school policies and practices.

- Half the English and two-thirds of Welsh LEAs claimed that their influence in promoting equal opportunities in primary schools had increased as a result of the reforms; a third believed that LEA influence had declined.

- Just under half of English but only one-third of Welsh LEAs believed LEA influence on equal opportunities policies and practices in secondary schools had increased as a result of the reforms: approximately one-third thought their influence had declined.

- A third of primary schools and nearly half of the secondary schools reported receiving INSET on equal opportunities from LEAs.

- Less than a fifth of primary and secondary schools in England and Wales reported receiving help on equal opportunities issues from LEA officers, advisory teachers and inspectors; less than one per cent claimed either to have received help from LEAs through coordinated school networks or financial assistance for equal opportunities.

- LEAs reported that since LMS their role in monitoring and training for equal opportunities had substantially increased. Approximately one-fifth of LEAs claimed to have been monitoring teachers and/or pupils or offering training for equal opportunities for schools prior to LMS. Currently, 90 per cent of LEAs claim to be monitoring pupil performance, and 80 per cent to provide equal opportunities training for governors and classroom teachers.

- One-third of secondary schools in England, half of secondary schools in Wales and one-fifth of primary schools in England and Wales reported receiving help with monitoring from the LEA.

- 70 per cent of primary and secondary schools claimed not to have had LEA-provided equal opportunities training for senior managers, classroom teachers or careers teachers.

- One-third of school governing bodies in primary and secondary schools were reported to have taken responsibility for monitoring gender performance in schools (the figures are lower in Wales).

OFSTED

- Over two-thirds of LEAs in the survey believed that OFSTED (using the original equal opportunities criteria) had raised the profile of equal opportunities in schools. Some LEAs appear to be actively helping schools meet the equal opportunities criteria, prior to formal inspection.

- Schools reported that in general OFSTED inspectors were requesting information on school equal opportunities policies/statements, curriculum, pupil performance and classroom practice; fewer had asked for information on equal opportunities in relation to sexual harassment, library resources or the pastoral curriculum.

Note: at the time of the research, no CTC had yet experienced an OFSTED inspection.

6   PERSPECTIVES ON THE EFFECTS OF EDUCATIONAL REFORMS

This chapter examines LEAs' and schools' perceptions of the impact of educational reforms on equal opportunities. The differential impact of particular curriculum, organisational and administrative reforms are considered in terms of their perceived positive or negative effects on gender equality. Examples are given of the ways in which headteachers, teachers and LEA officers, amongst others, have come to terms with the reforms and how they relate such government initiatives to their concerns about equal opportunities.

The first section of the chapter provides a brief context to how such reforms might be considered by schools. The second section offers a summary of how schools and LEAs in England and Wales have viewed specific reforms. The third and fourth sections give more detail about the reasoning which might lie behind such perceptions, first considering reforms affecting curriculum, assessment and monitoring, and then reforms affecting school administration and organisation.

6.1   THE CONTEXT OF SCHOOL REFORM

A range of factors have affected the ways in which recent education policies have impacted upon equal opportunities practice in schools. These include economic and geographic conditions, the history of individual school policy-making on equal opportunities, the levels of support previously experienced by schools, and the patterns of achievement already in place prior to the reforms. Other external factors, such as budget cuts, have also affected the ways in which schools have been able to tackle educational inequalities, whether amongst pupils or staff.

Taking budget cuts as an example of an outcome of the reforms which has appeared to have a profound effect on equal opportunities, it is clear that tighter financial constraints have severely limited such work. For example, at a North West LEA secondary school with falling numbers, staff have found it increasingly difficult to fill all the posts required under ERA with the school having lost 10 staff members (out of 50+) since April 1994, and being due to lose more in 1995. According to a long serving member of staff:

Staff have suffered from the drop in numbers. All are having to do more duties, they have difficult classes to deal with, with larger class sizes. When the school was larger, it was easier to 'swop' disruptive students around - now this is not possible.

The leakage of staff has meant that the member of staff responsible for gender recently had her responsibility extended to include all areas of equal opportunities.

Until the previous year there had been a B allowance, race relations coordinator in the school. Now, as no-one else is 'doing' race', she has been given the responsibility by default.
(Case study notes)

Other areas of this report touch on how the reforms have been experienced in the schools in relation to past histories of equal opportunities activism or lack of interest. Thus in inner city and/or traditional working class areas with a history of support for equality issues, the impact of the reforms is likely to have been rather different, and more negative, to that experienced in areas coming to such issues for the first time.

In the former case, the demise of the power of the local authority, and with it the ability to pursue (and fund) coherent policy development on equal opportunities, will be seen as a blow to widening gender equality. In the second instance, newly (through LMS) semi-independent budget-controlling headteachers and school staffs perceive new equal opportunities possibilities as they break away from low-spending local authority restrictions, for instance, by developing confidence-building strategies for female students or a more balanced curriculum for male students.

The outcome of the reforms and their impact on equality issues is thus likely to be patchy. In North West LEA, for example, officers regarded gender equality as currently less of a priority than previously, and more likely to be treated as but one aspect of equal opportunities generally. As schools were being let off the equal opportunities 'hook' so to speak by the withdrawal of LEA influence, officers were seeing very little evidence in secondary schools of genuine interest in equality issues, and at the primary level even less.

In contrast, for Shires County LEA, equal opportunities has rarely been a policy issue and, at school level, has been an equally forgotten or ignored area. Schools are now able, if they wish, to 'buy-in' to equal opportunities support services; however, 'uptake is very low indeed and courses barely take off. Equality is not seen as a priority in schools' (case study notes). In fact, the thrust of the authority's stance to equal opportunities is reflected in one primary head's view: 'if it is not an issue, don't make an issue out of it - let sleeping dogs lie'.

6.2   EFFECTS OF EDUCATIONAL AND RELATED SOCIAL REFORMS

The survey data reveal a complex picture of the impact of specific reforms on policies and practices.   The LEA questionnaire focused on a range of social and educational reforms, covering issues that might not be seen as strictly educational but may have had an effect upon gender equality in schools or on equal opportunities policies.   Here, the aim was to explore the effects of attendant policy developments such as the financing of local authorities through the community charge and/or council tax.

Table 6.1 lists the different reforms and their perceived effects on gender equality in schools, as measured on a four point scale from very negative to very positive.

The primary and secondary school surveys focused on specific educational reforms which were separated into two sets, those which affect pupil performance, achievement and standards (such as the National Curriculum, SATs and league tables) and those generating wider organisational changes such as LMS.   The aim here was to compare and contrast such reforms through questions relevant to the specific school context.   Thus fewer questions were asked of primary school respondents than secondary school respondents, the latter being additionally required to report on sector-specific reforms such as GCSE, TVEI, CPVE and work experience.

The case studies contributed to an understanding of the overall perceptions of the reform agenda, in particular by providing clues and explanations as to how perceptions are formed, and on what basis.   The overall effect of the curriculum reforms in terms of gender equality within the case study schools was also perceived as reasonably positive.   Even in the least thriving areas, some reforms were welcome, though the potential equality outcomes that were identified were possibly not those anticipated or planned for by the policy-makers.   Thus in a North West Community school, the head was of the view that:

> *The reforms have undoubtedly helped to put equality issues higher up the*
> *educational agenda, though certainly this has not been not prioritised or*

anticipated by government measures. The inclusion of equal opportunities in OFSTED inspections and in TVEI has been bound to have an effect. Also schools have had more independence to explore chosen priorities and there has been much more media coverage of equal opportunities issues.

Table 6.1   **Perception of LEAs of the impact of educational and related social reforms**

per cent

	Very Negative			Negative			Positive			Very Positive		
	E	W	E&W	E	W	E&W	E	W	E&W	E	W	E&W
TVEI	—	—	—	2	—	2	38	67	40	60	33	58
GCSE	—	—	—	17	67	20	76	33	75	6	—	6
National Curriculum	—	—	—	13	33	15	82	67	81	4	—	4
SATs	6	—	5	37	33	37	57	67	58	—	—	—
Publication of Exam Results	12	—	11	34	67	36	51	33	50	2	—	2
OFSTED Inspections	—	—	—	7	—	6	78	67	77	16	33	17
Increased Power of Parents	—	—	—	41	67	43	59	33	57	—	—	—
Parent Governors	—	—	—	32	67	34	63	33	61	5	—	5
Governing Body	10	—	9	48	67	49	43	—	40	—	33	2
Parent's Charter	16	—	15	36	33	35	48	67	50	—	—	—
Teacher Unions	—	—	—	6	—	6	72	67	72	21	33	22
LMS	18	—	16	60	67	61	23	33	23	—	—	—
Open Enrolment	13	—	12	65	33	62	23	67	27	—	—	—
Opted Out Schools	41	—	39	59	100	61	—	—	—	—	—	—
Community Charge	13	—	12	78	100	80	9	—	8	—	—	—
Council Tax	9	—	8	86	100	88	5	—	4	—	—	—
GNVQ	—	—	—	26	33	27	66	67	66	8	—	7
N	49	3	52	49	3	52	49	3	52	49	3	52

These have created an atmosphere where equal entitlement to all aspects of the curriculum is expected, particularly girls' access to the sciences. Publication of exam results has focused on emergent patterns of achievement.
(Case study notes)

Table 6.2   **The perceived impact of curricular and educational reforms in primary schools**

per cent

	Very Negative	Negative	Neutral	Positive	Very Positive
SATs	1	3	84	11	—
National Curriculum	1	1	60	38	2
Equal Opportunities as a Cross-Curricular Theme	—	1	44	48	7
Levels of Attainment	1	5	78	17	—
England and Wales N	390	390	390	390	390

Table 6.3   **The perceived impact of curricular and educational reforms in secondary schools**

per cent

	Very Negative	Negative	Neutral	Positive	Very Positive
SATs	4	9	72	11	5
National Curriculum	1	4	36	54	6
Equal Opportunities as a Cross-Curricular Theme	1	1	35	56	7
Levels of Attainment	2	9	68	19	2
GCSE	—	1	27	52	20
TVEI	—	—	14	56	31
CPVE	1	3	57	34	5
Work Experience	—	1	21	43	35
Other (e.g. GNVQ)	7	7	7	43	37
England and Wales N	235	235	235	235	235

One headteacher of a mixed comprehensive in a traditional working class area experiencing relatively high levels of local unemployment and relatively low GCSE results, confirmed his deep commitment to giving all pupils a chance.

> *Society works so much against working class kids in terms of being able to access higher education, being able to afford A-levels, the negative experiences parents had in their own schools. All these sorts of things.*

This school had tackled such class inequalities in a variety of ways. Additionally, gender issues had been addressed through the development of a whole school policy on gender which, for example, dealt with the promotion of women in senior management, the use of teacher appraisal and classroom observations, newly defined home - school liaison schemes, annual departmental reviews and reporting of gender in relation to pupil achievement. Interestingly, the response of the head of this school to the effects of the reforms was also largely positive.

> *The educational reforms?... It's an interesting conundrum in that fairly much - I cannot speak for all staff - but generally the reforms the Conservatives brought in terms of the ideas, I think we would support nearly all of them. However, the implementation of them has been appalling. LMS, National Curriculum and associated assessment. Being rigorous about assessment and the changes to parent preference for schools. The raw league tables say nothing about the value that has been added to the provision of education within individual institutions. So in terms of parents knowing our exam results it is absolutely rubbish and vital....it has got to be presented in a way which is fair to schools....*
>
> (Case study notes)

For the remainder of this chapter, the reforms are grouped into those affecting curriculum, assessment and monitoring, and the cluster of reforms related to the administration and organisation of schools. Data from the survey and the case studies are reported under the appropriate headings as follows.

6.3   CURRICULUM, ASSESSMENT AND MONITORING REFORMS

In the LEA survey, seven specific reforms were identified (i.e. TVEI, GCSE, National Curriculum, SATs, GNVQs, OFSTED Inspections, Examination League Tables) which had aimed either at changing curriculum and examinations or improving pupil performance and standards. Significantly, all seven were viewed by LEA respondents as having positive rather than negative attributes.

This generally positive response to the reforms was also evident in the school surveys where a major feature was the neutrality or relative popularity of the reforms concerning testing, cross-curricular policies and the National Curriculum in terms of promoting gender equality. Secondary school respondents were positive towards the introduction of newer vocational qualifications such as TVEI and GCSE. What now follows is a brief overview of perceptions of individual reforms.

TVEI

In 1984, the Manpower Services Commission (MSC) identified sex-stereotyping as an obstacle to educational progress, and with respect to TVEI (at that time, under its jurisdiction), announced a criterion for funding, that:

> *Equal opportunities should ne available to people of both sexes and they should*
> *be educated together on courses within each project.*
> (MSC 1984)

As a consequence, from 1984 onwards, the development of equal opportunities policy and practice has been a key criterion for funding. Additionally, LEAs have played a central role in monitoring and evaluating local schemes. At the time of the research, TVEI (in its main and extension phases) had been in existence for over a decade and had earned the reputation as a major initiator of equal opportunities policy activity (McIntyre 1987, TVEI 1991, NFER 1993).

Thus the research showed that TVEI was felt to have been positive in 40 per cent and very positive in over half (58 per cent) of the English and Welsh LEA responses and appeared to have few detractors among secondary schools. This positive view towards TVEI was replicated in the case studies; thus in Home Counties LEA, TVEI had a considerable impact in raising awareness of gender issues, particularly in the absence of LEA coordinated initiatives. In North West LEA, a TVEI curriculum coordinator with responsibility in the local scheme for equal opportunities, had made an enormous effort to keep the issues afloat in the LEA.

There is a TVEI Focus Group meeting each term which addresses the four main local TVEI themes: equal opportunities, guidance, teaching and learning and work-related issues. The 54 schools in the scheme are required to send a representative to each meeting which covers the four topics. A report goes to each school annually based on returns from a questionnaire on Performance Indicators. An annual report to the main TVEI distils the information from all the reports; and following this, targets are set for the following year.
(Case study notes)

The account offered by individuals involved in TVEI varied considerably, however. For example, at a meeting of 15 TVEI School Equal Opportunities Coordinators (14 female and one male) in Welsh Urban LEA, many pointed to their lack of status as slowing up the change process. Comments as follows were fairly typical: 'I've got no pull with older senior colleagues and though in meetings they nod and agree, getting things done is quite slow'.

Some reported behaviour from colleagues that was sexist and bordered on the verge of harassment. In the case of a female equal opportunities coordinator working in a boys' comprehensive school, a male teacher was reported as saying 'An equal opportunities coordinator in a boys' school is daft - we don't need it'; and others were involved in what can only be termed name-calling:

In our school the men call our equal opportunities working group 'the knitting circle'. There's lots of antipathy to it and most of our male colleagues are convinced it's a group striving to win the women staff some promoted posts.
(Case study notes)

Others reported more success though necessarily, it seems, with support from senior management.

I was surprised at the staff's response to the Head's equal opportunities initiative - you know teachers, they can drag their feet...but he pulled together a team representing most curriculum areas and largely they've done some good work which has been valued by the majority of staff.
(Case study notes)

In fact, the efforts made by individual coordinators did not go unnoticed or unappreciated by the schools involved. The value of the work of one particular coordinator (in North West LEA) was described by a secondary head as follows:

> *TVEI has had a strong impact on awareness of equality issues in the school....As gender coordinator appointed in 1985...[she] created a climate of recognition of gender issues. She originally made a big impact in the school although there were three or four members of staff who were actively resistant. They have since left the school. Generally the staff has become more consciously egalitarian.*
> (Case study notes)

Some TVEI schemes have been responsible for providing guidelines on monitoring equal opportunities, usually based on the guidance document *Framework for Inspection of Schools* (OFSTED 1993b). In additional, in North West TVEI, guidance was geared to changing curriculum and pedagogical practice drawing on materials from *Genderwatch* (Myers 1992) and the Runnymede Trust's *Equality Assurance* (1993). Alternatively in Home Counties TVEI, the approach was more linked to audit and monitoring as the following introduction to the guidelines indicates:

> *This audit document aims to take into account the full range of Equality of Opportunity in the contexts of race, disability and gender. The document is designed to combine the monitoring of existing practice with the continuing for Equality of Opportunity. This entails bringing about change through individual, departmental and whole school/college planning.*
> (Case study notes)

In Shires County, TVEI was the reform most frequently cited as a catalyst for equal opportunities initiatives, especially where funding enabled the release of staff to develop curriculum materials and to develop monitoring procedures.

GCSE

GCSE was also seen as largely positive with 75 per cent in the LEA survey claiming to be positive (and 6 per cent very positive), though with a minority of respondents (20 per cent) having negative views. Over 70 per cent of secondary schools and 75 per cent of CTCs reported overall positive effects of GCSE on gender equality. Likewise, evidence from the case studies suggested that the introduction of GCSE has been viewed as benefitting girls, perhaps due to its emphasis on course work rather than examinations. As a male head of a comprehensive put it: 'GCSE tends to lend itself to the ways in which girls like to study. Girls have been able to produce their best work over time.'

The introduction of GCSE was also generally seen as marking a watershed in changing examination patterns for 16-year-olds and providing a more balanced profile of subjects particularly for girls. However, some were cautious about the impact of GCSE, and its relationship to overall standards and other qualifications such as A-level. As a North West secondary head put it:

> *Exam results at GCSE level could have been predicted from screening tests for*
> *pupils on entry to the school. However...[he] detects a big gap in academic*
> *level between GCSE and A-level. GCSE is not a very effective preparation for*
> *A-level studies.*
> (Case study notes)

The introduction of GCSE appeared to benefit girls in two additional respects. First, the incorporation of new subjects for girls in the curriculum seemed advantageous particularly for high achieving girls.

> *Brighter girls and boys want to keep science options open (for veterinary,*
> *medicine, engineering). The school's option system is now designed for students*
> *to take three separate sciences at GCSE or a dual award.*
> (Head of Science, case study notes)

Second, the increased emphasis on data-gathering to compare standards across schools and LEAs has resulted in an expanded focus on girls' patterns of achievement, in particular, on GCSE results at Key Stage 4. The following comment from a CTC senior manager was fairly typical, though in this case the proportion of girls and boys gaining five GCSE (A-C grades) was higher than for most other case study schools.

> *Currently [it was reported] girls are out-performing boys: roughly speaking,*
> *45.4 per cent boys are gaining five A-C GCSE grades, compared with 61.5 per*
> *cent girls - though it must be remembered that this is still the comprehensive*
> *intake going through the school with the more selective banding.*
> (Case study notes)

National Curriculum

The introduction of the National Curriculum was seen to have been positive in 81 per cent of the LEAs and very positive in a further 4 per cent, with only 15 per cent viewing its introduction in a negative light. Sixty per cent of secondary school respondents and 75 per cent of CTCs identified the National Curriculum as a significant advantage, in comparison to the primary school respondents of whom only 40 per cent reported positive effects. Primary schools appeared relatively neutral about the effects of the National Curriculum and cross-curricular themes relating to gender equality. However, a large percentage (97 per cent) of schools claimed that policy-makers had *not* explicitly addressed the issue of gender equality in the National Curriculum; and to the question of whether the introduction of the National Curriculum has altered the contents of specific subjects between 1988 and 1994, an overwhelming majority of secondary school respondents claimed that there had been 'very little alteration'.

The case studies nevertheless revealed a strong base of support for the National Curriculum as a means of extending gender equality. For example, in both primary and secondary schools in North West LEA, it was claimed that National Curriculum implementation had been an important awareness-raising exercise. A primary head suggested that it 'has made staff focus on the fact that all activities should be open to all children. This has alerted them to equality and gender issues'.

A secondary head likewise suggested that the National Curriculum had resulted in a broadening of the curriculum so that, for example, all pupils at the school take Double Science, and that some cross-gender choices in options are evident:

> *Currently of a set of 17 students doing Home Economics, 14 are boys - possibly in order to enter the services or the catering industry. More specifically, it is ability rather than gender that dictates choice of lower status subjects.*
> (Case study notes)

In London LEA, compulsory elements for both boys and girls, especially Science and Technology, were deemed 'a good thing', though it was suggested by a secondary head that schools in the authority were indeed ahead of the reforms:

> *The curriculum is aimed at ensuring equal opportunities. 100 per cent of pupils are entered for Double Science. In years 7-9 all children do Textiles and Food*

Technology. [However] more boys are doing Design and Technology for their
options at the moment but this is not always the case.
(Case study notes)

Compared with other National Curriculum subjects surveyed and discussed, Technology emerged as an area of considerable controversy. Seen originally as substantially enhanced and rendered more accessible to both sexes when it was included as a key subject in the National Curriculum (compared say with the previous CDT curriculum), the post-Dearing changes incorporating greater choice at KS3 were viewed with some concern. For example, it was noted in Midlands LEA that:

Allowing options at KS3 has meant that traditional patterns are reemerging.
[The] majority of girls opt for Food Technology. Child Development remains
almost exclusively a girls' subject.
(Case study notes)

Similarly, the Shires County Coordinator for Educational Business Activities expressed the view that whilst schools had been keen on Technology and IT before the Dearing Report:

Everything is about to change post-Dearing. We are going to see the
introduction of vocational education in years 10 and 11.
(Case study notes)

In her view, the re-introduction of curriculum choice pre-16 was likely to result in the re-emergence of subject stereotyping and narrowed options for girls in particular.

Meanwhile, as we have seen above, whereas Catering is now frequently taken by boys and girls - in a mixed High School in Welsh Urban LEA 15 boys and 21 girls had opted to study catering - traditional CDT gender divisions seem to be re-emerging. For example, in the same High school:

Only six boys compared to 33 girls opted to study Textiles; this is a reduction
on last year when eight boys studied the subject.

Whereas 43 boys study Graphics only 13 girls selected it. This has resulted in
one male-only class and another with 16 boys and 13 girls attending.

Product Design attracted 34 boys and only seven girls, again resulting in a male single-sex group of 20 pupils for this new Technology option.
(Case study notes)

Physical Education was another curriculum area which was frequently perceived as having an explicitly equal opportunities dimension at both school and LEA level, in particular, in articulating differences in viewpoint about appropriate sporting activities for each sex and the form of masculinity (and femininity) promoted in various sporting activities. For example, in an admittedly sports-dominated urban Catholic junior school with otherwise no apparent interest in gender issues, there was a girls' football team and sporting activities were organised frequently on a mixed-sex basis (e.g. gymnastics, athletics, cross-country).

In contrast, in the relatively more prosperous Shire Counties, LEA cricket appeared as one of the key differentiators of male and female pupils in some primary schools, with netball remaining as 'only for the girls'. In the context of curriculum entitlement, the issue of primary sports stood out as a symbolic statement of local concerns about appropriate male and female spheres. Parental values were cited where mixed-sex activities were not provided:

The boys wouldn't want to do it. They're conditioned by the time they get to us about what they're expected to do. Somebody in the staff room just now was talking about casting for the infant pantomime - parents might not be too happy if boys were asked to be fairies....I think they look a bit worried that a fairy might stick.
(Case study notes)

An interesting and different point made by an officer of Midlands LEA was that with the introduction of the National Curriculum, parents are less likely to criticise activities consciously designed to challenge stereotyping.

The National Curriculum means that most parents now assume that their children will have to do everything and so complain less at non-stereotypical activities.
(Case study notes)

113

The case studies also revealed considerable support for the concept of 'entitlement'. This is more fully discussed in Chapter 7.

On the downside, there was some cynicism about the extent to which government curriculum reforms had made any genuine difference. To quote a teacher in London LEA, 'very few changes have been made because of government. PHSE (Personal, Health and Social Education) continued even though it is not a National Curriculum subject'.

Moreover, it was also noted by case study researchers that a 'hidden' or more covert set of curriculum practices was still very much in evidence. For example, in a Welsh classroom, the following observations was made by the researcher, despite existing school equal opportunities guidelines:

> *The teacher concerned seemed to lack awareness. His two occupational examples were gendered (Policeman and Fireman)....The 'hidden curriculum' was operating in this lesson in subtle ways...One message that the teacher conveyed was that year 10 pupils were not involved in decision making.*
> (Case study notes)

SATs

As we can see from Table 6.1 SATs drew relatively positive responses from the LEAs surveyed with few viewing the effects of SATs negatively (5 per cent); though rather less enthusiasm was forthcoming from the survey schools where most adopted a relatively neutral position on SATs. Except CTCs with nearly half being positive. In the case study schools, few of which had recently implemented SATs testing due to the teachers' boycott, perceptions were also mixed. In primary schools, assessment was seen to be enormously time-consuming but helpful in providing data on individual and patterns of performance across subject areas. SATs results were used in London and Midlands schools to monitor race, ethnicity and social class alongside gender as components of equal opportunities. In one London primary school, a spin-off from this kind of monitoring of achievement was that teachers were further exploring *why* certain groups were failing by carrying out school-based research, i.e. using questionnaires and interviews with pupils.

However, it was also claimed that the new forms of assessment had not necessarily made teachers more aware of gender inequalities, since they had already been made aware of any inequalities at the level of the classroom through previous LEA-provided INSET and increased general understanding of such issues. In other schools where there was little knowledge of gender issues, the introduction of SATs also seemed to make little difference.

GNVQs

On the whole LEA survey respondents were reasonably positive about GNVQ and its impact on gender equality (66 per cent positive, 7 per cent very positive) although 27 per cent were rather more negative. However, because of its relatively recent appearance in the government reform process (at least at school level), it drew fewer and less enthusiastic responses from the school surveys and was rarely mentioned as an issue within the case studies. However, the head of a mixed comprehensive in a mainly white, working-class area on the fringe of North West LEA noted a recent shift post-16 with the main growth point being increased take-up of GNVQs rather than A-levels:

> *The expansion of the sixth form has parallelled the growth of vocational offerings at 16 plus viz GNVQs. The sixth form currently has 90 students: 60 in first year and 30 in the second year.*
> (Case study notes)

Reforms to the Careers Service and guidance

The impact of various local careers services and teachers on raising the profile of issues of gender equality in schools (often in conjunction with vocational education projects and schemes such as TVEI or work-placement programmes) emerged as one of the unanticipated findings of the project. For example, Midlands Career Service appeared to take pride in its monitoring of student destinations - it claimed to be the 'first in the country to be able to say what students are doing at 16+'.

In contrast, the focus in Home Counties LEA has been in promoting awareness among staff. Thus, ED targeted funding had encouraged (and facilitated) the development of work on gender in the form of an 'excellent' *Gender Training Manual* published in 1991 which focused on raising awareness, improvement in practice and promotion of equal opportunities, and gender-fair recruitment, retention, and staff development practices. According to the area careers officer, the response of the LEA was typical of its entrepreneurial ethos:

The Department of Employment also indicated that equal opportunities was one of the areas it was prepared to support and identified it as a topic in the development scheme of the Careers Service. The LEA had bid for the money therefore as well as bidding for other themes.
(Case study notes)

Not surprisingly, at school level, career teachers who adopt equal opportunities as part of their wider brief, place greater emphasis on student attitudes and self-perceptions. A careers teacher and school TVEI coordinator in a North West Catholic comprehensive argued that his input was important in order to raise the self-esteem of his pupils.

Careers material is vetted for equal opportunities purposes. The Council's equal opportunities policies are used since the Council is a large provider of work placements...[He] has found that in terms of exploring careers information, bothgirls' and boys' aspirations are well below their capabilities. Students 'undersell' themselves.
(Case study notes)

Data collection and monitoring

Data collection and its consequent emphasis on performance and competition, appeared to have had a varied impact in the surveys and across the case studies. In London LEA, for example, data collection was seen as having been made more complex post-ERA, with the loss of the Research and Statistics branch alongside the Inner London Education Authority (ILEA). In contrast, for other local authority areas, data collection had become easier or at least more systematic during this period. Thus girls' improving performance levels, at least up to GCSE, had become better known. The perceived reasons for this shift, even in previously male-dominated subjects such as Science, are illuminated by the views of a male Head of Science at a North West Catholic comprehensive, who:

found that the girls did extremely well in their examinations last year. For Physics which he teaches, of the five who gained grade A (of 25 entrants) in GCSE, four were girls. At present, the sixth form is very small with few science entrants. In his view, the reasons why the girls did so well was that they worked hard, responded to the course and deserved to succeed. [He suggested that] at 16, girls are sometimes more mature than boys.
(Case study notes)

116

In his view the subject had also changed, which has encouraged more interest from girls:

When...[he] started teaching 10 to 12 years ago, there was a heavy emphasis on boys doing Physics as they wanted to become Mechanics and Engineers. Fewer of these opportunities are now available, so now students are now taking the subject for different reasons. Brighter girls and boys want to keep Science options open (for Veterinary, Medicine, Engineering)...Girls are choosing Science because they see themselves as 'workers' and also because traditional jobs are no longer available.
(Case study notes)

In terms of the effects on gender equality of introducing Examination Tables, responses to the LEA survey (see Table 6.1) were fairly evenly spread with 52 per cent positive or very positive and 47 per cent negative or very negative. However, reactions at case study level were more frequently hostile, seeing the introduction of 'league tables' as effectively antithetical to the promotion of gender equality. For example, in the possibly more aware ethos of London LEA, at least in terms of equality issues, it was claimed that the limitations to league tables, publication of results etc. were that they did not really help teachers in their classrooms. It was also argued that the introduction of league tables had led to structural rather than pedagogical solutions to improving practice and performance, and that this might have detrimental consequences for girls' continuing success.

The pressure to get good exam results tempts schools to go towards streaming. But streaming would lead to segregating the sexes as there would be mostly girls in the top stream and a sink class of boys at the bottom.
(Case study notes)

Interestingly, in a selective highly successful girls' school which had achieved one of the top league table rankings in the country, the press attention given to the school in the national and local press had negative effects on the girls themselves. They were most concerned about the fact that they were seen to have an unfair advantage over their friends in local schools. They did not like the image of their school and of themselves - 'Lesbian, stuck up, work all the time, all pass their GCSEs and taking five A-levels' as one girl described it. They were all expected to be 'of a certain standard' and, in one case, a pupil had been told that she had been successful in gaining a (part-time) job working behind the till in a health food shop because of attending a 'top' school. She was worried about the unfairness of this.

OFSTED inspections

OFSTED inspections attracted substantial support in the LEA survey, with 77 per cent of respondents claiming to be very positive and a further 17 per cent positive. OFSTED also attracted support across the case studies. The inclusion of criteria for equal opportunities was viewed particularly positively (confirming the trends discussed in Chapter 5). For example, in Shire County, for which gender equality had been a low priority in the past, it was made clear to schools that they needed to prepare for the fact that OFSTED inspectors were looking for separate targets for equal opportunities. Schools were advised to make sure that department policies had an equal opportunities statement, and that resources needed to be chosen carefully to avoid gender and racial stereotyping.

Similarly, an OFSTED inspector based in Home Counties LEA claimed that by including equal opportunities in the criteria for OFSTED inspections to which each inspector was obliged to adhere, OFSTED had been important in raising awareness - though application was uneven. She suggested that:

> *There were particular aspects that they [inspectors] would focus on - efficiency, equal opportunities, special needs and curriculum quality. Every inspection, when one tended for it, had to include these elements, but obviously each inspector could decide how much time was given to each of the areas. You could decide that equal opportunities did not have much time.*
> (Case study notes)

In fact, in that particular county, such use of inspection criteria to promote gender equality seems to have been spectacularly successfull, as the case study notes report:

> *School after school referred to OFSTED reports which they had analyzed carefully. They were clearly aware of the need to present their approach to equal opportunities in a positive light and some primary and secondary schools were having to draft their policy statements overnight in preparation for the inspection.*

Though there are some differences in the requirements of OFSTED and OHMCI (for Wales) as was noted in Chapter 5 - according to a Welsh primary advisor the accompanying documents have provided a similar thrust and 'motivation' for heads and governors to do 'something' about equal opportunities.

The patchy application of OFSTED criteria on equal opportunities was, in fact, a frequently highlighted feature of the project. For example, lack of understanding on the part of some inspectors was viewed by a Midlands LEA officer, as part of her perception of a wider downgrading of gender as an issue:

> *OFSTED inspectors sometimes do not understand equal opportunities well enough to make informed judgements on what they see. Fewer governors [are] now coming to training on issues to do with race and equality. Personnel has placed greater emphasis on ethnicity. Gender [is] not seen as a priority in Council as a whole.*
> (Case study notes)

However, an OFSTED Inspector from Home Counties LEA was rather more positive although she acknowledged that equal opportunities practice was patchy, sometimes superficial and a low priority:

> *She found that equal opportunities was patchy maybe, but she had not produced any damning statements about equal opportunities for any particular school. Schools, she felt, had to change. They showed some concern, but they were not tackling it deeply enough in her view. It was not so much negligence as the fact that other priorities were taking pride of place.*
> (Case study notes)

Significantly, the 1994 OFSTED Summary Report on the secondary schools inspected in Shires LEA highlighted the fact that only approximately half of the schools had a written equal opportunities policy, and that these were superficial and needed development: 'Most schools had positive statements of intent, but, in many cases, practice failed to acknowledge and celebrate differences and value them equally' (OFSTED 1994). In particular, the report identified the need for further in-service training to support teachers in translating awareness into strategies for classroom organisation and management.

The next section considers perceptions of the cluster of reforms aimed at redistributing the organisation and funding relationships between schools and LEAs.

6.4   REFORMS CONCERNING THE ADMINISTRATION AND ORGANISATION OF SCHOOLS

Parents and Governing Bodies

The greater involvement of parents in the life of schools was viewed positively by almost two-thirds of the English and Welsh LEA survey and negatively in four out of ten instances. Parent-governors were felt by 66 per cent of LEA respondents to have had a positive or very positive impact whilst only a quarter felt that they had been a negative force in the promotion of gender equality.

In contrast, the impact of Governing Bodies on equal opportunities was viewed rather more negatively, with 42 per cent of LEAs responding positively and more than half (58 per cent), negatively. In fact, evidence from the case studies suggests that discrimination by governing bodies is now a matter of some concern. For example, in North West LEA:

> *Considerable concern [was] expressed (by LEAs) over governing bodies viz quality of governors, status differences between governors, power of the head, gender inequality in composition of governing bodies and chairs of governors. Governors are now much more likely to discriminate; and there has been little take-up of offers of equality training.*
> (Case study notes)

One of the reasons for this apparent pessimism about how governing bodies are approaching equality as part of school policy is the under-representation of women and minority ethnic groups as members (more fully discussed in Chapter 7).

A question on the *Parent's Charter* was included in the LEA questionnaire to which responses were fairly evenly divided. However, it was not an issue that generated much debate and indeed, it did not feature as a reform of any significance across the case studies.

Local Management of Schools (LMS)

The impact of LMS on gender equality was perceived negatively or very negatively by more than three-quarters (77 per cent) of LEA survey respondents and positively by only 23 per cent. In the case studies, LMS was generally seen as a threat both to equal opportunities and to enhancement of policy development within the schools. For example, the personnel officer in London LEA was extremely concerned about the impact of LMS:

> *The personnel services are working hard on gender, race and disability equality policies. Because of LMS, however, we cannot force schools to implement the good practice we recommend. We try to get good practice and have drafted a code of practice for governors - but we cannot enforce it.*
> (Case study notes)

Similarly, officers in North West LEA expressed feelings of powerlessness with the advent of LMS, in that they felt unable to raise the gender profile, though Council policy on gender had become more formalised in recent years (with the appointment, for example, of a designated officer).

Creation of City Technology Colleges (CTCs)

The CTCs which responded to the questionnaire tended to be more positive than the secondary schools about the educational reforms. In particular, they were more enthusiastic about SATs and assessment procedures more generally, and the National Curriculum. They were also positive about GCSE and the introduction of work experience programmes, though rather less so concerning TVEI and CPVE.

As already noted. CTCs had a relatively high questionnaire response rate, with respondents claiming to be providing a high level of support for equal opportunities. They also claimed to have actively developed college policies on equal opportunities, although under no formal obligation to do so. Five schools had developed equal opportunities policies early on in their existence (one in 1987, one in 1989 and three in 1990) and four between 1990 and 1994. The case studies revealed some limited but interesting insights into the new cultures of the CTCs, with their emphasis on the creation of quasi-commercial organisational practices and ethos.

Some of these practices drew student criticism about the narrowing of the curriculum, for instance in concentrating on Technology and Commerce rather than on the wider curriculum including the Humanities and Arts. Other features of the CTC school ethos which drew criticism (from students) include 'strictness' and 'utilitarianism'. This emerged from interviews with sixth form girls in a case study CTC. It was reported that a number of working class girls had left the CTC prematurely because they were 'bored' (a feeling also expressed by the students present) and 'sick of school' and its strictness - though this might well be a common feeling among students as they come to the end of their school life. Those who had left early included three girls doing Chemistry in mixed classes who felt over-pressured to keep up with the boys.

However, an alternative view offered by staff was that because of the relative greater emphasis on Science, Mathematics and Technology, and better facilities, some subjects were able to span the gender-divided curriculum: thus, 'boys can now study Food Technology, and more girls are specialising in Science and 'heavy' Technology.' (Case study notes)

As the head of careers put it:

> Becoming a CTC has helped improve the motivation of girls towards a number of traditionally non-female subjects such as Science and Technology. Before the CTC, both schools were poorly equipped: now they have excellent facilities for all aspects of Technology especially CDT (as was). A policy decision has been made to concentrate KS4 provision for Technology on the girls' school site and KS3, on the boys' site. This policy has helped to underpin the notion of absolute equality between the sexes in such subjects.

However, the extent to which subject choice and interest in Science and Technology had changed was less evident. The head of careers admitted to seeing shifts in some subject areas (e.g. increased entry into Business Studies for boys and girls, and Medicine for girls) but not in the 'harder' subjects of Science or Technology. The head of Science in the same CTC similarly reported little evidence of growing female student interest in Science and Technology:

> There is still a lot of interest in banking and in the law - in particular Afro-Caribbean seem to want to be lawyers. White, South London girls tend to be more traditional: the more middle-class, the more important is a girl's career. Working-class girls do not have the same level of aspiration.

Open enrolment and Grant Maintained Schools (GMS)

The impact on gender equality of both open enrolment and opting out were viewed negatively in the LEA survey. Open enrolment was welcomed by only 27 per cent of respondents whilst the effects of opting out were viewed negatively by all LEAs (61 per cent negatively and 39 per cent very negatively). The case studies revealed the extent to which grant maintained status is unequally distributed across LEAs. In the case study LEAs, relatively few schools had opted out.

122

In Midlands LEA and in North West LEA no school had, as yet, opted out although a North West LEA primary school had begun negotiations. In North East LEA, three primary schools had become grant maintained, though no secondary school to date. In London LEA, grant maintained status had not generally been sought: only one primary school had opted out (and there was also one CTC). Grant maintained status was unevenly spread across the rural shires and home counties. In Home Counties LEA for example, four secondary schools had become grant maintained out of a total of 42. In contrast, Shire County LEA which had encouraged GMS had more grant maintained than LEA secondary schools.

Survey responses included 26 from secondary and two from primary grant maintained schools in England. This represented a higher response rate from grant maintained schools than from LEA maintained schools. Of the 26 grant maintained secondary schools, 21 had been county schools and five had voluntary status in 1984. However, the relatively small scale nature of this reform makes it difficult to establish the effect of opting out on gender equality or equal opportunities activities.

Nevertheless, schools in the case studies indicated the complexity of factors affecting grant maintained schools. Single-sex status, admissions policies and selection procedures, the effects of LMS, the publication of examination results and league tables in competitive local markets, have all shaped grant maintained schools' approaches to equal opportunities. Two selective schools in the case studies (one each for girls and boys) suggested an awareness of the importance of equal opportunities policies in a competitive environment. Focus was placed on broadening male and female education not just emphasising academic performance: a reflection perhaps of the fact that in these schools, students were selected from the top three per cent of the ability range. Both headteachers stressed the importance of equal opportunities issues by highlighting the hidden curriculum, staffing structures, and providing students with confidence to engage with non-traditional spheres.

Not surprisingly perhaps, examples of the benefits of opted-out status for gender equality were forthcoming from GMS staff. For example, one GMS head, who had previously worked in a LEA mixed comprehensive with a highly interventionist strategy on equal opportunities, had appreciated the value of local authority involvement to help weaker pupils. However, in the context of her highly selective GMS girls' school, grant maintained status within a largely laissez- faire LEA had 'freed her up' to develop strategies for her female pupils unhindered. She claimed that she could not blame the LEA which had to set its own priorities more suited to other forms of pupil intake. Thus, her school had been able to develop entirely new strategies to assess, monitor and develop girls' extra-curricular activities (e.g. musical events, clubs, hobbies) in order to improve self-confidence. Girls were assessed on their participation, achievement, responsibility and leadership in these activities. The school had further created a new set of pupil responsibility posts and developed strategies to encourage independent learning and, more specifically, the exceptionally able female pupil.

Equal opportunities coming from the centre, she argued, was not the way forward for her school. Convinced of the 'speed, depth and commitment of staff within the school', which in the LEA-controlled days had been 'shackled' (especially by strategies that she described as 'honeypot budgeting'), the combination of LMS and GMS, she felt, had provided greater opportunities to develop an ethos and a commitment within the school involving all the staff.

Interestingly, whilst GM schools tended to celebrate their increased independence, in Shires County LEA those that were single-sex appeared to downplay the popularity of single-sex education on the part of parents, who were seen as being more concerned with the performance and development of the 'whole child', and also about the lack of male teachers at primary level:

> *Single-sex education was less of a current priority of parents in comparison with performance and the development of the whole child. Some schools and the OFSTED inspector argued, however, that the presence of single-sex schools reflected back on primary school parents who were keen to encourage similar [single-sex forms of] organisation in terms of subject and sports.*
> (Case study notes)

Thus a male primary head in the same county (Shire LEA) recalled:

> *Parents of a year-5 girl pupil had commented to him that she had never had a male class teacher. They wanted her to experience a male teacher by year 6…They asked if a male teacher could be provided. Pupils should have the benefit of both sexes. The Head had never met such a request from parents of sons.*
> (Case study notes)

Additionally, the effects of a high percentage of GMS schools in an area meant that comprehensives had to fight hard to keep their high ability pupils, especially if GMS schools were highly selective, single-sex and using grammar school traditions (uniforms, traditional teaching styles etc.). Secondary heads were well aware of the competition and had to take decisions about whether to provide single-sex sports, more symbols of the grammar school ethos, or to cater for high numbers of pupils with special needs etc. For some this was not of great significance, particularly if the school already had a firm image of itself within the community it served. For others, it might act as a brake on possible equal opportunities developments (e.g. in developing mixed-sex sports).

The importance of recruiting students to the school, especially to the mixed sixth form, appeared not only to have raised awareness of parental concern about girls' confidence in the outside world but also about boys' attitudes to women. As the head of a boys' grant maintained commented:

> *Some boys tended to treat women staff abominably but then they treated their mothers even worse.*

This lack of respect for women was linked to boys' previous experience in primary schools, and also with concern about secondary school staffing structures and the culture of male school sports. Anti-bullying policies, the introduction of girls into hitherto all-male sixth forms and changes to the pastoral curriculum were all used to address these perceived problems. Yet at the same time, work experience placements tended to reinforce sex-stereotypes.

However, in the main, the perception in Shires LEA was that the league tables and 'an aggressively competitive market for pupils among GM grammar schools' had not led to any emphasis on differences in male and female performance: rather the focus had been on the importance of building girls' self-confidence, of educating them for leadership, and in encouraging a 'softer masculinity'.

Community Charge and Council Tax

Similarly, the impact of the two other local authority organisational changes unconnected directly to education - the 'Poll Tax' and the subsequent Council Tax - were seen in the LEA survey to be negative for equality issues in 92 per cent and 96 per cent of cases respectively, while positive responses were few and far between. However, these were aspects of the reforms which attracted little comment from case study schools or the LEAs.

Teacher Unions

Whilst the teacher unions have not been a force in the creation and implementation of the government-led reforms, as the main representative bodies for teachers, their guidance and advice has been sought and assessed by many in the profession. In the main, the work of teacher unions in relation to equal opportunities has been viewed as reasonably helpful and positive, as indicated in the 72 per cent of the LEA survey who were positive about the role of trade unions in promoting gender equality, with a further 20 per cent claiming to be very positive - in all over 90 per cent responding positively.

The role of the unions and the stance towards the reforms has been complex, though realistic. The following account of the views of a teacher union representative was fairly typical.

> *As a teacher and a trade unionist, [he]...is upset by the 'insularity' being encouraged nationally. He is fighting to keep... [municipal] services, to get value for money by sharing services. 'Equal opportunities units are the first to go' when cuts are applied. In his view, Margaret Thatcher was right to 'set about education': changes were needed. However, the degree and rapidity of change and the extremes (viz allowing such independence of governing bodies) have put enormous strains on schools.*
> (Case study notes)

In Midlands LEA, the influence of the unions in the past had been quite important in terms of equal opportunities: for example, a decade previously the local National Union of Teachers (NUT) had carried out a study on the work histories and promotion of men and women in primary schools which was acted upon by the LEA. And in 1985, the NUT pushed for and won an extended period of maternity leave for women teachers. However, it was felt that more recently trade union activity on equality issues has been less marked.

6.5   CONCLUSIONS

Curriculum, assessment and monitoring reforms

- The changes to the curriculum, monitoring and examinations, whether academic (such as the National Curriculum) or vocational (such as TVEI), and the monitoring of pupil performance and standards through OFSTED and data collection, were seen to have had largely positive effects on the promotion of equal opportunities.

126

- TVEI was seen as positive by nearly all the secondary schools in the survey.

- GCSE was seen as positive by three-quarters of LEAs and by 70 per cent of secondary schools in England and Wales.

- The National Curriculum was seen as a positive reform in terms of gender equality by 85 per cent of LEAs, and more positively by secondary schools (60 per cent) than by primary schools (40 per cent).

- SATs were perceived as potentially having positive outcomes for equal opportunities by 60 per cent of LEAs, though 84 per cent of primary and 72 per cent of secondary school respondents gave more muted responses.

- GNVQs had a mixed reception with only 27 per cent of LEAs seeing the new qualifications as having positive effects for equal opportunities.

- LEAs also gave a mixed reception to examination tables, with 52 per cent claiming to be positive and 47 per cent negative. OFSTED, in contrast, attracted mainly positive responses, although the case studies indicated a rather cooler response from schools.

Reforms relating to administration and organisation of schools

- The LEAs considered most of the administrative reforms of schooling to have largely negative consequences for equal opportunities and gender equality more specifically.

- Open enrolment was seen as positive by only 27 per cent of LEAs (most were negative - 62 per cent); and *all* LEAs considered the effect of grant-maintained status to be negative for gender equality.

- LMS was perceived by 77 per cent of LEAs as having predominantly negative effects on equal opportunities.

- CTCs appear to want to be associated with equal opportunities policies and have better facilities for Science and Technology. However, there are no early indicators of changed gender patterns in subject choice or in take-up of scientific or technological careers.

- The role of trade unions in equal opportunities was seen as positive or very positive by a large majority of LEAs.

- The effects of the imposition of community charges and the council tax on strategies to promote equal opportunities through LEAs were overwhelmingly considered to be negative or very negative, though this was not an issue of particular importance in the case studies.

7   CHANGING GENDER CULTURES

This chapter focuses on the current gender relations of primary and secondary schools, and LEAs in England and Wales. Interviews with local education authority officers, advisors and inspectors, and teachers and students in schools yielded insights into changing school cultures as well as issues, concerns and strategies currently being used to extend equal opportunities.

The chapter focuses on four themes: the language of gender; management and school cultures; issues of concern; and practices, projects and initiatives on gender currently being developed.

7.1   THE LANGUAGE OF GENDER

The ways in which gender issues are being framed and discussed in schools and LEAs currently take a variety of forms, some of which are directly related to current political and educational priorities. Thus the emphasis of specific approaches might differ quite markedly, as shown by the following examples.

Value-added as equal opportunities

'Value-added' is increasingly being used to show the difference the school makes in a child's learning, as identified through entrance and exit levels of performance. For example, a Value-Added Unit was established by Welsh Urban LEA in 1994 to provide 'a detailed analysis...[so that] schools can make informed decisions about the resources at their disposal'. Thus data on pupil performance (GCSE, A- and AS-levels, Reading and Non-Verbal Reasoning at 10+ and socio-economic data) have been collected over time to provide information for school improvement. Rules for the use of data included maintenance of confidentiality, promotion of professional discussion, access to information, publication and monitoring and evaluation of developments.

Similarly, in a girls' selective GM school which has utilised the Newcastle University VA analysis, a value-added approach has been used more individually as:

> *Measure[ing] each pupil against her own previous achievements, thus differentiating between individuals with varying talents. It is then possible to target support accurately to the needs of the individual.*
> (School document for 1993-4)

129

Value-added analysis has also been applied more managerially, as a useful tool for identifying good and bad teachers 'distinguishing between the effectiveness of different teachers within a department and of different departments within the school'. (Case study notes)

However, some schools have felt it inadvisable to use the actual term 'value-added' with students, possibly for fear of introducing extra jargon. For example, in one case study school, two alternative phrases were used: 'The GCSE predictor for A-level grades' and 'On the basis of your GCSE results you have the potential to get at least a...'

Raising Standards as Equal Opportunities

In attempting to raise standards and examination results, a number of schools in the case studies were clearly addressing equal opportunities issues but by another route. Thus, in a London LEA mixed comprehensive, a number of mini-projects had been carried out as a means to raise achievement levels. These included exploration of collaborative styles of working in the light of the tendency for girls and boys 'to choose to work separately and in different styles'; 'how to get the boys to work more like the girls'; having a record of sexist as well as racist incidents; developing non-sexist careers literature etc.

At a primary school in London LEA where the problem of boys' poor reading had emerged as a 'standards' issue, one approach was to reorganise the school library so as to make it more appealing to boys by introducing more non-fiction. However, one of the teachers interviewed for the project was unconvinced about this strategy.

> *'If you observe the boys reading non-fiction and fiction they are looking at the pictures, not reading'. She is wary that conclusions...[about boys' preferred reading]...may not be applicable to their own boys and girls.*
> (Case study notes)

Teachers at the same school also considered pupils' groupings in the classroom with great care, regularly seating girls next to boys and organising classroom activities for mixed- or single-sex groups as appropriate.

Rights and responsibilities as equal opportunities

This version of equal opportunities has appeared as a means of involving parents and the community. For example, in a nursery and infant school in a 'deprived' area North East LEA,

130

the aim is 'to encourage people to be assertive rather than aggressive, to know their rights and responsibilities'. Embedded within this approach is the concept of 'effective citizenship', and features of this approach include: a weekly 'good work' assembly; rewards systems to reinforce self-esteem; rights and responsibilities formulated as a cross-curricular theme; and governors' guidelines. Rights and Responsibilities Statements in the school policy suggest extrinsic and intrinsic motivational factors linking standards to equality issues, for example:

> *You have a right to quality education.*
> *You have a responsibility to learn effectively.*
> *You have a right to full and equal shares in school activities.*
> *You have the responsibility to do your best and support others.*
> *You have a right to be treated with respect.*
> *You have a responsibility to respect others.*
> (Extracts from the school statement)

Entitlement and inclusivity as equal opportunities

'Entitlement' is a term initially identified as a right within the National Curriculum and is increasingly being substituted for equal opportunities. Typically, a Home Counties LEA Coordinator for industry and business suggested that whilst TVEI had been linked to equal opportunities, it should not be singled out. According to her, everything the authority does contributes to increasing equality, although the interpretation, as a concept, 'was closer to entitlement'.

Another aspect of entitlement or inclusivity can be found in the claim often made that gender cannot be seen on its own as an equality issue. For example, in Midlands LEA it was seen alongside ethnicity - 'Asian girls have a different set of equal opportunities problems than white girls' - and social class which 'comes through as an important factor in influencing achievement and aspirations'. Also in terms of disability in Midlands LEA:

> *In the Deaf Unit... the issues were a little more complex. Most of the students were Asian and their deafness placed them in a minority within a minority...Issues to do with gender which the teachers were aware existed were hard to tease out from a complex set of factors.*
> (Case study notes)

131

Similarly, in a North East LEA infant school, gender was viewed as part of the school and community context.

> *The gender issue here is seen very much in terms of the particular circumstances of the school and therefore in relation to poverty, lack of rights, sense of worthlessness. The school encourages and rewards assertiveness (rather than aggression) in relation to rights and responsibilities.*
> (Case study notes)

Equal opportunities as add-on or integrated

Equal opportunities appeared, in different schools and LEAs, to be taking contradictory positions. On the one hand, a secondary school in Midlands LEA was writing an equal opportunities policy for the first time (prompted by an OFSTED visit) in order 'to prevent it from being pushed out by other pressures'.

> *[The] perception here [was] that whereas in the past equal opportunities could be trusted to be part of everyone's brief (through INSET and general awareness) and not the responsibility of a single equal opportunities officer, now it needs to be rescued with focused action.*
> (Case study notes)

In other case study schools and LEAs, identified post-holders signified that equal opportunities already had a reasonably high priority. A typical LEA post-holder for equal opportunities was a primary advisor who had been allocated an equal opportunity responsibility three years previously on top of his original workload following 'several requests from female county councillors' and other pressures on the Director of Education to create an equal opportunities post-holder.

> *In a sense when I was asked to do it - I was already in post. With equal opportunities this happens a lot. People just get it added to their job. But anyway I was happy to work on it...I am the token white male (laughs) typical isn't it - the worst possible scenario isn't it...It had to come from some push from Labour County Councillors.*
> (Case study notes)

Another variation of this role was an LEA advisory post for 'Angular Issues', an apparently rag-bag job which included the LEA's remit for the inner city, bilingualism, adult and youth services, travellers' provision, racial and sexual harassment policy etc. However, other schools and LEAs adopted more integrated approaches, for example, as in the Midlands LEA school where a new policy was being developed to reflect an overall change in the way the school conceptualised its mission. In this case, equal opportunities was incorporated into all school policies.

A similar perception of equal opportunities was held by a seconded primary teacher for equal opportunities in North West LEA funded through TVEI. Her 'personal belief [was] that equal opportunities underpins everything in school and that there is potential to tackle it in most subjects'. Strategies mentioned include:

- *single-sex and mixed-sex groupings;*
- *talking activities: turn taking and listening skills;*
- *English: talking about texts, the language writers use;*
- *developing girls' logical thinking;*
- *in history and geography: woman's role and the absence of women from accounts;*
- *advertising and the role of women and ethnic minorities;*
- *stereotypes and non-traditional roles;*
- *rewriting fairy stories;*
- *involving parents by setting homework which involves discussion e.g. questionnaires;*
- *regular planning of how teaching will address equal opportunities.*

(Drawn from case study notes)

7.2   THE CULTURE OF MANAGEMENT

One of the most worrying features to emerge from the research has been the evident continuing dominance of white male cultures in school and LEA hierarchies. A quote from a male headteacher usefully illustrates the perceptions of LEA management held by some, as: 'grey suited men running the authority in a paternalistic rather than partnership sort of way' with 'blunt autocratic reputations' and with 'uncomfortable, defensive, dismissive, sceptical, [and] hostile' responses to gender issues.

In fact, in the secondary school survey more than three-quarters of the secondary heads (and two-thirds of CTC principals) were male. In the primary school survey, slightly over half the primary school headteachers were male. The Welsh surveys had a higher proportion of male headteachers in both primary and secondary schools.

Whilst these findings may be viewed as skewed in favour of males, they constitute a movement away from a starker gender imbalance of headteachers 10 years ago, in particular in the case of primary schools - although data for this period were frequently incomplete.

Significantly, it was also found that the gender balance of the current chairs of Governing Bodies also favours males. In the case of both primary and secondary schools (and CTCs separately) the chairs of governing bodies are male in about three-quarters of the cases. (These data were not available for 1983-4.)

Similar patterns of (white) male over-representation were also apparent at virtually every level of organisation within the case study LEAs and schools. In only one of the seven LEAs visited was there any satisfaction expressed about staff issues (in London LEA where there had been a long history of equal opportunities awareness and policy initiatives). Explanations commonly offered for the low level of interest in gender equality issues within LEAs, drew attention to the lack of movement and over-representation of male staff in the senior management of schools and LEAs.

Apart from schools in the two LEAs with a strong and continuing tradition of equal opportunities policy-making and development, both of which had a presence of women at senior management level (although still a minority), the prevailing management cultures across the other case study areas were almost exclusively male and white. A typical mixed-sex secondary school might have, to quote an example from the case study notes:

> *A senior Management Team [which] is largely male and white head, two deputies (one male, one female), four senior teachers (male). Heads of Department are mainly men and pastoral posts have mainly gone to women (3 out of 5).*

In another such school the headteacher blamed the lack of women at senior levels on long-term staff patterns:

The school ethos of equal opportunities unfortunately is not reflected in the staffing structures of historical reasons. Some staff had been at the school for a long time.
(Case study notes).

Such inequitable staff patterns have been even more noticeable, according to a senior member of staff at a CTC, where catering and support services have been 'contracted out'. Thus, because of the need for schools to keep a tight control of their finances, equal opportunities tends to become more of a luxury rather than a requirement. As was noted by a female member of the senior management team:

The biggest draw-back with respect to equal opportunities...is lack of black staff. She has noticed that whilst virtually all the academic staff are white, all the cleaners are black and most of the catering staff are black (though the head caterer is white). Because the college manages its own finances, its priorities have been to contract services to the lowest bidder and concern for quality rather than concern to eliminate poor wages and conditions.
(Case study notes)

In a number of cases reported to the project, the white, male management culture has led to an ethos antithetical to women staff. For example, in a Shires primary school:

In a culture where staff are called 'Brains', 'Sergeants' and 'Ladies', women teachers felt uncomfortable and out of place. Many I [the researcher] spoke to were aware in a quiet way of gender issues but had failed to find opportunities to develop strategies in the school. They had come across issues in training or on INSET courses...Few of the teachers had... a chance to discuss this work in staff meetings. They did not feel 'listened' to generally and were aware therefore that gender issues were unlikely to be discussed either.
(Case study notes)

It seemed that within such male management cultures, approaches to gender issues could be dealt with in a number of ways. They could be ignored altogether or as one advisor described it in respect of a number of primary schools, equal opportunities could became a 'twilight zone'. Or gender issues might be deemed irrelevant - for one largely male management team, the position taken was 'why make an issue of something that is not an issue'. Yet in the same school, female staff had identified parental concern about boys becoming too effeminate; and were concerned

135

themselves about girls not gaining sufficient access to the computer, girls and boys underachievement in maths and English respectively and significantly, the lack of respect (and promotion prospects) accorded to female staff.

In other male school cultures, gender equality had become absorbed into the language and rhetoric of the school but had not made an impact on policy or ethos. Thus, for example, when required to provide an equal opportunities policy statement prior to an OFSTED visit, one headteacher asked the LEA for help in the form of 'drafted paragraphs'. In this case, he had little sense of how equal opportunities might be integrated into overall school policy or into the school's development plan.

Not surprisingly, therefore, discriminatory practices in recruitment and job interviews continue to flourish - as a female member of staff found when she applied for the post of deputy. She thought she did a very good interview and was told that she looked 'gorgeous'. However, she did not get the job which went to a 'fairly unremarkable' male colleague because she was apparently 'more pastoral' and the school, its was claimed, needed a disciplinarian.

In a number of the secondary case study schools (though not in the project surveys), sexual harassment emerged as a specific area of concern that attracted some discussion about how best to go about encouraging potential complainants to seek help rather than to find their own solutions. This led, in a coeducational comprehensive in London LEA, to the development of a separate policy on sexual harassment which defined appropriate terminology, created new forms of equal opportunities offence, provided a new system of recording such offences and identifiable action.

7.3   CHANGING STUDENT PERCEPTIONS AND SCHOOL CULTURES

There appears to be a clear trend of increasingly positive attitudes towards girls' schooling. In terms of gender differences in performance, 64 per cent of respondents from the secondary schools survey claimed to have noted that girls are increasingly out-performing boys at various assessment levels, a claim that has also proved a major feature of the case studies. However, primary school respondents were not nearly so unequivocal with 49 per cent denying evidence of any gender difference and only 17 per cent reporting girls' higher achievement levels.

Evidence from the case studies suggests that parents have also changed perceptions of girls' educational opportunities. As a deputy head in Shires County put it:

> *You get very few parents who say it's not worth girls doing that [staying on] or girls going on in education, but the recession has helped that because lots of families are resting on the female income now.*
> (Case study notes)

Changing student perceptions

Such awareness of changing labour market patterns has also been reflected in comments from students. A Personal and Social Education (PSE) female teacher noted the changing values in working class communities as follows:

> *There is great awareness in the classroom of the breaking down of barriers, about what is a traditional girl's job or boy's job. Actually, if you ask the question, they will see no problem with girls wanting to be bricklayers or whatever. Whether that actually affects what happens in reality...*
> (Case study notes)

Consequently, girls (from all social backgrounds) appear to see achievement at schools as of benefit to them in the labour market and in their future lives. Even in areas of high unemployment where stereotypical perceptions of male and female roles continue (as in areas of North East LEA) 'women are increasingly taking on both the childcare and working roles'. Thus, girls see a twin future of childcare and occupational opportunity, though eventual jobs are often in low paid and low status areas and they are well aware of the obstacles preventing them escaping from stereotypes. As a female student from a working class background put it: 'the boys have got stereotypes of women and women have got stereotypes of women. Men prefer women to wait on them hand and foot'. (Case study notes)

The role of men within the family seems to be particularly problematic for some girls. For example, whilst the career aspirations of a group of ten-year old girls in a Catholic Junior School in an area of high unemployment, *viz* gymnast, secretary, lawyer, lifeguard, detective, lawyer, footballer, and nurse, might be thought of as fantasy rather than to do with labour market reality, several challenged existing stereotypes and their view of the role of men in their future lives was instructive, to say the least. They suggested for instance that:

> *Men could be on drugs - [you] can't trust men to be there all the time. [You] can't trust men full-stop...[They] don't see future lives as staying at home to look after children... [They had] all sorts of ideas...about how to look after children when working.*
> (Case study notes)

Significantly, as the researcher noted, the girls seemed very practical and focused: 'very independent and unromantic/unsentimental'.

At secondary school age, girls seemed to be more motivated than many of the boys. As a headteacher put it: 'girls now have ambition and employers are beginning to see them as reliable and employable. Girls don't see any forbidden areas as in the past'.

There are also indications of an emerging generation of 'new' boys and girls, conscious and supportive of equality issues. Interviews with students suggest that while attitudes of many male (and to a less extent female) adolescents remain traditionally narrow and stereotyped, the new generation has a larger share of more confident girls and 'softer' boys. An illuminating instance of a new 'caring' male generation was a 17 year old (from London LEA), who in reflecting on the CTC's longer school day and its ethos, argued that the longer day might be dangerous for young students in the darker months of the year. He also expressed concern about the apparent downgrading of the 'softer' humanities in the CTC's avowedly commercial environment, suggesting that it would be detrimental to the curriculum balance offered by the school (although he, himself, was currently occupied with technological subjects).

This trend was confirmed by a secondary member of staff (in the same London LEA) who reported noticing that a group of 'softer boys' seemed to be emerging from the primary schools 'no doubt influenced by much of the equal opportunities that has gone on in the local borough'. And, in an LEA in a different part of the country, the promotion of a 'caring, creative masculinity' was the concern of one head of a selective GM boys' school who was at pains to break through traditional sport-centred competitive masculine codes in his school.

Interviews with, and observations of, male and female students also emphasised their acceptance of the idea of the importance of women in the labour market, especially with endemic male unemployment in some parts of the country and the formation of dual career families in other, more prosperous areas. As the researcher of Shires LEA noted: 'In secondary schools pupils seemed to be aware of the need for women to earn a living, especially in the context of economic recession'. However, she also noted that it was 'only a few girls though [who] were actively considering a range of non-traditional occupations (noticeably not often in engineering or industry) and seemed confident of success'.

Boys appeared to accept the need (or perhaps the inevitability of) 'working wives' although for most the issue of childcare remained vague and unresolved. For girls, childcare appears to becoming incorporated into a wider sense of possibilities and opportunities for them in the future, at least for the higher-achievers.

An illuminating example of girls' changed perceptions (and perhaps what it means to be British) came from second-year sixth-formers of the CTC in London LEA in response to questions about their future. The first notable difference from former decades was the increasingly multi-ethnic nature of many urban schools. The group included L (Chinese, born in Vietnam moving to Ireland and then to Britain in 1988); S (Nigerian, born and brought up in the UK); A (of Singapore/Glaswegian origin); and C (Ghanaian, born and brought up in the UK). The researcher was told by the head that this was a typical group of upper-sixth students at the school.

On leaving school, all four in the group were intending to go to university and into jobs. In response to being asked what they might be doing in 10 years time, their answers, extracts of which follow, suggest that a shift has taken place in (some) girls' view of their future lives.

C - [expects] *to study biochemistry, and then into the private sector. Might have a husband and child.*

A - [expects] *to study English. She was not sure what she might do after that, perhaps travel, writing, teaching. Does want to have children though is not sure whether she wants to get married.*

S - [expects] *to study law, psychology, and then to work for a 'big firm'. She would not be married nor have children in 10 years time. She might have children in her 30s but first wants to own property.*

L - [expects] *to study media studies, journalism, and then go o newspaper industry, journalism. She eventually wants to get married and have several children (her mother had 12 children).*

While their aspirations were high, they were also aware of continuing blocks to their progress. For example, they still feel that girls are not perceived as quite equal to the boys in the college though 'boys let girls do more things' than in the past. Also, the Foundation Company of the school still has ceremonies and events from which women are excluded and those that do include women are heavily male dominated.

Single-sex and coeducational schools

Whilst not a main feature nor a prominent debate during the reform period, the value or otherwise of single-sex compared to mixed-sex schooling continues to be a perennial concern, in the press at least. Interestingly, the conventional notion that parents want their daughters to go to single-sex secondary schools and their sons to mixed schools did not emerge as a major feature or trend in the research.

For historical reasons a number of Church schools in the case studies were single-sex (in London and North West LEAs in particular) and because of the grammar/secondary modern legacy, some single-sex comprehensives which had previously been selective, still managed to maintain their elite ethos. In the main, the case studies showed that high performing single-sex schools, whether selective or comprehensive, church, local authority or GMS, were very popular with parents. According to the head of a selective girls' school in Shires County:

> *Pupils come from as far afield as neighbouring counties, travelling miles because of the reputation of the school. What attracted them was not just the academic performance but the extra curricular opportunities, responsibilities given to girls at school, the careers programme and Higher Education access.*
> (Case study notes)

Coincidentally, two schools at the top of the league tables were located within the case studies but in different LEAs. Both of the schools were selective (one by default) and single sex (one each for boys and girls), though the boys' school had introduced girls into the sixth form mainly, it was claimed, to retain overall numbers.

In fact, in the three instances in the case studies where there was single-sex secondary provision up to 16 for boys' and mixed sixth forms thereafter, it was noticeable that the integration of girls proved far more problematic where the process was not handled sensitively. In one such school in North West LEA, discussion with female first year sixth-formers raised the following issues:

Boys dominate in the school...[and] pretend they know much more than they do. Girls felt inadequate until they found this out.

Science teachers tell the girls what to do, [and are] much more directive to them...

In [a] Politics class, [there is] awkwardness for the only girl in the group. The teacher makes an effort but it's 'embarrassing'. One girl was sure she was marked higher because she is a girl.

...the only girl in a Physics class...feels very embarrassed. The boys continually make sexist comments.

Boys tend to be more immature...[when they have come from] a single-sex environment...

There are not enough women teachers. Only one student said she...[had been] taught by a woman. As the girls came to the school to get good results... they need confidence. 'Boys act as though they are god'. [It is] difficult for girls to come out of their shells.

...[The girls have the] impression that many teachers feel that girls 'lower the tone' of the school.

(Extracts from case study notes)

7.4   PERCEIVED AREAS OF CONCERN

A number of new areas of concern relating to equality issues emerged during the project. One of the most common has pointed to an apparent loss of motivation amongst working class and black *boys*. It was claimed time and time again that as traditional areas of male employment have collapsed or altered, working class (and/or black) male students, now tend not to see themselves as benefitting academically or vocationally from schooling. They therefore appear to be less motivated than girls, and more alienated from the classroom. Further, whilst working class boys seem increasingly to stay on into the sixth form, they tend to study for vocational qualifications such as GNVQs (rather than A-levels).

In North East LEA, special schools placed particular emphasis on boys with language difficulties (boys are consistently over-represented in such schools) and secondary schools have attempted to tackle the fact that boys seem less able to cope with more informal systems of schooling - 'They [boys] can get on if someone stands over them but otherwise they are not as mature as girls and discipline problems arise...Boys find it less easy to sustain a level of effort.' (Case study notes)

In Midlands LEA, concern about boys' underachievement, particularly in reading and language, has led to the requirement for a shift in practice from some teachers.

The teachers...who had had a long involvement with equal opportunities issues were reluctant to devote too much to boys, because it will weigh against the still unresolved issues around girls' education. However, their action plan resulting from OFSTED inspection has highlighted the achievement of boys as an area of concern. This appears to be less driven by equal opportunities issues as by the need to raise the overall performance of the school.
(Case study notes)

The underachievement of white boys, in particular, was identified in the OFSTED inspection of a Midlands LEA comprehensive. In its response the school accepted that external factors led to underachievement, such as local unemployment, though it also identified behavioural, disciplinary and academic reasons. After some discussion the recommendation was:

That we move away from looking at the underachievement of boys, to looking at the disruptive behaviour of a small minority of mainly white boys which affects the achievement of the majority.
(School discussion paper)

For middle-class areas and in particular, for selective boys' schools, English (particularly Literature) was perceived as the weak point in boys' curriculum profile. For example, in a Shires LEA boys' school 70 per cent of whose pupils gained A-C grades at GCSE, only 30 per cent of the boys achieved such grades in English.

The head put this pattern down to the failure of the examination boards to reward the particular forms of male creativity and literary styles. Course work too seemed to cause difficulties even to these boys. [However] by changing to a different examination syllabus with less course work, he was able to bring the English Literature results in line with the pattern in other subjects.
(Case study notes)

A concern related to boys' general under-achievement has been the apparent over-representation of boys in disciplinary procedures and in exclusions. In Midlands LEA it was noted that disruptive behaviour primarily stemmed from a minority (though significant number) of boys and that 'the concentration of the failure of poor white boys was potentially dangerous'. Similarly, from the records of a London LEA primary school over two years, the head noted that the proportion of boys relative to girls kept in at play-time for disciplinary reasons, was 90 per cent and 97 per cent respectively. He also expressed the view that girls tended to be punished more severely by teachers than boys for misdemeanours - 'it happens that a well-behaved girl is severely punished when she is a little less well-behaved'. Yet again, in a high school in Welsh Urban LEA, exclusion numbers particularly for boys, seemed to be on the increase - from 17 boys and three girls for September 1993-July 1994, to 25 boys and two girls for September 1994-February 1995.

However, there also remain what have been termed 'unresolved problems' for *girls*: for example, the hidden curriculum still appears to produce girls with low self-esteem and confidence - 'girls creating themselves as boys want to see them'. And schoolgirl pregnancy and the general destabilisation of families and communities, rarely mentioned in equal opportunities terms, were also identified as 'unresolved' issues.

Other, additional, issues of concern were what a Home Economics Advisor (and OFSTED inspector) termed as 'fire fighting issues'. These included for Home Counties and Shires LEAs respectively: girls and trousers and boys and earrings at secondary level; and the separation of boys and girls on the register, mixed-sex toilets and competitive sports at the primary level.

Also, for those involved in arranging and evaluating work-placement schemes for years 10 and 11, apprehension was frequently expressed about the sexism, racism and/or traditional expectations of *employers*. In one LEA, these all came together when, after interview, Asian girls were refused work placements. Apparently the employers perceived the girls as culturally stereotypically over-compliant and obedient. Given the schools lack of 'clout' with such employers, the schools opted to work with the young women in helping them to perform better at interview.

On the staffing side, the relative lack of good *male primary staff*, was another issue of speculation and concern. For example, a Shires LEA primary head reported that 'the number of male applicants [for teaching jobs] had "dried up" and there were few male student teachers'.

His view was that children needed to be taught by men as well as women, particularly lower down the school, but that parental pressure had pushed male teachers in his school towards the upper age range.

> *It is my belief that children should have access to a variety of teachers, but basically at some stage within the primary school they ought to have been taught by men as well as women. We did try the experiment of moving Mr. X down the school...he did a very good job but from parental pressure, wanted him back in Year 6 because he is so good there.*
> (Case study notes)

What then seemed to be happening is that when male teachers were appointed, they tended quickly to be promoted to management posts. This has resulted, in one LEA, in the perception of a further down-grading of women teachers' expertise:

> *Female primary teachers were distressed by what they felt to be an antagonistic male culture in the school. They expressed concern at the indifference to female teachers' needs, a lack of interest in their professional viewpoints, and a patronising attitude to them as women.*
> (Case study notes)

7.5   PRACTICES, PROJECTS AND INITIATIVES

Case study visits revealed a range of initiatives and positive practices showing how issues are being taken forward into the new circumstances and conditions created by the reforms: at the level of the school, the LEA and with involvement of other bodies. In some cases, the values/social justice dimension of the first wave of equal opportunities (in the 1980s) and the standards dimension of the second wave (post-1988) appear to have fused together to produce new forms of policy-making and innovation. For instance in the case of a CTC, past history and present structures have come together both to re-create policy and to aid recruitment:

> *The head of PSE carries responsibility for equal opportunities across the college. There was a long-standing equal opportunities group in the girls' school which continued its work after CTC status, then involving staff from the*

boys' school which had no such group. The 'mixed' group together with students updated the earlier policy and created the colourful equal opportunities poster which is very visible around the school and leaflet for the school brochure.

(Case study notes)

Most of the initiatives being developed in schools and LEAs were not widely disseminated even within any one authority. Thus documentation on, and descriptions of, these initiatives were only available from the school or authority directly involved.

School initiatives

(i)   Personal and Social Education: Gender Module (Shires LEA)

One of the few places in the school curriculum where equality issues can legitimately be discussed is in the cross-curriculum area of Personal and Social Education, and a number of schools had developed supporting materials for this. Here, the school had developed a module which aimed to address equal opportunities and to 'offer differentiated tasks within Careers work in PSE'. The contents of the module included discussion of stereotyping, prejudice, sex-roles, 'acceptable gender occupations', and was principally designed to 'encourage students to think about their skills and interests when making career choices and to consider areas of work traditionally associated with the other sex'.

A variety of teaching and learning strategies were employed for the module including group work, brain-storming, debates and whole class discussion. 'Differentiation' or recognition of differences between pupils was acknowledged in:

- inclusion of a wide range of teaching and learning styles (as mentioned above);
- degree of autonomy and choice for pupils;
- supported self-study;
- choice of presentations by pupils;
- use of study guide.

The school had allocated two teachers (part-time) to develop the materials, who extensively researched the range of resources on the topic before designing the module for the PSE curriculum.

(ii)   Anti-Bullying Policy (Shires LEA)

One of the more recent extensions of equal opportunities work has been in the area of bullying and harassment. A number of case study schools had developed anti-bullying policies, viewed also as embracing anti-sexist and anti-racist dimensions. In this case, the school policy document suggested that bullying may take different forms, for example:

- hitting people and other general examples of physical abuse;
- using threatening behaviour;
- theft and deliberate damage to other people's property;
- teasing, name calling and psychological taunting;
- creating an environment of fear;
- ignoring and ostracising individuals.

One of the features of the policy is a formal procedure for dealing with any incidents once reported: for example, interviewing the victim to ascertain emotional, psychological and physical effects; a meeting convened with relevant parties ('colluders and bystanders'); the possible involvement of parents; solutions on how to deal with the matter identified and action plan put into place; a review of any decisions in the light of subsequent changes and developments.

(iii)   Co-educational High School: single-sex Science experiment (North West LEA)

This particular initiative did not originate from concern about gender inequality, but rather it aimed 'to diffuse confrontations and promote good relationships between pupils themselves and with staff'.

It originated in the Science department of the school and focused on year 9 students, as 'a confidence builder or rebuilder'. Half the pupils in the cohort were directly involved in the experiment, being divided into single-sex groups, and half remained in the mixed-sex control group. The teachers changed groups over the year so that each class was able to have a mix of male and female teaching styles. On evaluating the initiative, the single-sex groups remained positive although the mixed control group was fairly negative about the experiment. At the time of writing, the experiment is in its early stages though teachers' perceptions were that:

> *The all-boys class is less confrontational and less noisy than a mixed one would*
> *be. There is not a huge rush to get apparatus and there is less flexing of muscle*
> *for the girls and competition towards them...The teacher of the all-girls class*
> *found them great to teach; she had to spend far less time telling [them] off.*

Interviews with the pupils involved suggest that many were not quite sure why Science was chosen for the experiment:

> *Though they had a general idea of what the experiment was about and boys*
> *confessed to thinking they're 'boss'. Two girls thought Science was chosen*
> *because it was the kind of subject which required consultation in groups. In the*
> *all-girls' class there was a sense that a lot more work was getting done.*
> (Case study notes)

(iv)   High School initiatives for girls (Welsh Urban LEA)

In 1994, the above school embarked on a range of initiatives specifically to support the teaching and learning of girls. For example, the school welcomed the WISE (Women into Science and Engineering) bus during the Spring term when all pupils were being asked to think about their 'options' for year 10. Female pupils in years 9, 10 and 11 were also provided with the time and space to talk to the staff and to consider non-typical careers in science and engineering.

> *'We try to arrange for male and female staff to deliver option talks to year 9*
> *pupils' reported a female deputy head who, herself, took part in these sessions:*
> *as an engineer, she could act as a positive role model for girl pupils.*
> (Case study notes)

Another initiative, organised by the Careers' Department was the 'Take Our Daughters to Work' (TODW) scheme in April, in which a group of girls from the school took part. Some accompanied parents and friends, arranged on an individual basis, whilst a large group of year 9 girls spent the day with a local construction company. The deputy spoke of the value of such initiatives and the importance of 'work experience tasters' whereby both girls and boys experience non-traditional occupational settings: 'Breadth and balance of the National Curriculum...can be interpreted to include breadth in work experience placements'. Such experiences, she argued, can be utilized and recorded, for instance, in work experience diaries and/or on a Record of Achievement summative report at the end of year 11.

(v)   Mixed Comprehensive: strategies to address boys' underachievement (Shires LEA)

This school, in a traditional working class catchment area and fairly low down the league tables (20 per cent gaining 5+ GCSE A-C grades), perceived two main areas of underachievement: working class male students with little interest in academic subjects, and girls' lack of interest or achievement in Science. There has clearly been a deep commitment from the whole school to equal opportunities, and among other strategies, 'all sorts of mechanisms' had been instituted to tackle boys' lower academic performance, particularly in English. These include:

- Careful supervision of homework with teachers making thorough checks.

- Senior management involvement in cases where homework has not been completed, with 'family work' reviews and the setting of attainable targets.

- Review of students' test scores on entry to the school (at 11+) with the aim of raising teacher and parental expectation.

- Development of language and reading skills through small group teaching and highly structured activities.

- Experimentation with a variety of more effective teaching styles, for example, devoting more attention to differentiated work in the classroom.

- Widening language activities for boys, for example, by encouraging them to join a travelling drama group or dance group, or to engage in public speaking.

- Making the improvement of boys' performance levels in English a target for all staff involved including the English department, senior management or student-teachers.

- Placing the emphasis in careers advice on students continuing their education post-16 and considering the possibility of non-stereotyped occupations.

- Careful evaluation of students' progress at the English departmental annual review, and in the broader monitoring of staff patterns and students' achievement levels, and in the appraisal of teachers' performance in the classroom.

Initiatives at LEA level

(i)   INSET on monitoring equality in the Primary School (Midlands LEA)

This one-day session was structured to show primary school staff ways in which they might use the collection and analysis of data to inform practice in their schools. Staff from schools actively involved in monitoring were invited to share their experiences with participants. For example, a primary deputy head reported how he was able to use his analysis of KS2 pilot results and KS1 teacher assessments to raise meaningful questions.

One of his main findings was that at KS1, while girls achieve at Level 2 in the core subjects, there was a fall off in their performance at Level 3. At KS2, more girls achieved at Level 3, but there was a fall off at Level 4.
(Case study notes)

This led to questions within the school concerning 'a comfort level' beyond which girls seem unwilling to commit themselves. Other issues discussed at the session included playground behaviour difficulties, the development of speaking and listening skills, classroom management and strategic planning.

(ii)   Governor training on equal opportunities (Welsh Urban LEA)
The authority had been one of the first to develop a governor training module on equal opportunities. Through developing a 'pool' of school governors willing and able to deliver training, the authority was able to provide support for governors, not only on equal opportunities, but on other topics such as discipline and bullying, the National Curriculum, how to run meetings and salaries.

Coming from a variety of backgrounds, each of them [the trainers] has in common a commitment to the education of our children and a belief in the value of governor training.
(Extracts from brochure)

Praised by researchers from the University of Warwick for good practice and for the positive evaluation of participants, take-up for the module by governors nevertheless appeared to be quite low.

As the County equal opportunities advisor observed:

The trouble with governor training is you can't impose it on them. Governors will ask you to lay on some training for them to do the INSET they need...but take-up varies.

(iii)   Management Opportunities for Women INSET Course (Welsh Urban LEA)
This initiative came from the need to respond to County Councillor requests that women teachers should receive positive career training, and was a 2-day course targeting women in middle management in secondary schools. The first day of the course took place early in the school

year, concentrating on: the internal and external barriers to women in management; 'how we are successful and how we hold back'; stress management and designing a curriculum vitae. The second session took place early in the Spring term with an agenda largely set by the participants. During the three years of its existence, 46 women from 41 schools had participated.

General initiatives

(i)   TVEI School Coordinator (Welsh Urban LEA)

As we have seen elsewhere in this report, TVEI has been one of the major advocates of equal opportunities during the reform period. The role of the school-based teacher TVEI coordinator has therefore been a particularly important one. How have these roles worked?

At an observed coordinators' meeting in Welsh Urban LEA, it was reported that TVEI had given coordinators the time, materials and contact networks (with similarly positioned equal opportunities coordinators from other schools). One outcome of this was 'a sense of camaraderie among them as they talked about their work in this role', noted by the researcher. This information network had enabled coordinators to suggest initiatives in their own school from an informed base: 'He [the Head] does listen and we've "borrowed" a couple of ideas from other schools'. Thus the coordinators were able to report the following outcomes and achievements of their work:

- All schools were on an alphabetical roll.

- 75 per cent of them had contributed to the writing of equal opportunities policies - others were developing them.

- Three schools had designated responsibilities for equal opportunities monitoring to departments in their school.

- Two schools had erected equal opportunities notice boards in their staff rooms.

- Two schools had launched an 'equal opportunities week' with thematic assemblies.

- Three schools had held whole school Art competitions to design logo posters pertaining to equal opportunities.

- Four schools had made requests for members of their Governing Bodies to train on the County's equal opportunities training module.

- Six schools were monitoring option choice in year 9 and scrutinizing examination results by gender.

- Eight schools had sent middle management women staff on the County's 'Management Opportunities for Women' INSET Course.

- One school was offering single-sex science option courses for year 10 pupils.
  (Case study notes)

(ii)   Guidance on equal opportunities in preparation for inspection (Home Counties LEA and TVEI)

Sets of such guidelines were in existence in several of the case studies. For Home Counties TVEI, the development of an Equality of Opportunity Audit had been identified by the County TVEI Team as one of its key areas for development for 1993. It resulted in a 16-page booklet designed to assist schools in measuring their progress in the area of equal opportunities against the criteria listed in the OFSTED (1993b) *Framework for the Inspection of Schools*. The booklet was designed to be used initially by the headteacher and senior management, and then to be read more widely, as a discussion checklist for Departmental and staff INSET. It was left to each school to decide on the most constructive way of identifying the strengths and weaknesses of its current provision, as well as actions to be taken to ensure that the school satisfied the inspection criteria.

The booklet identified a number of factors in terms of equal opportunities: policy documents, intake and exclusion patterns, pupil grouping arrangements, curriculum content and access, classroom management and teaching, resources, pupils' achievement, pastoral provision, school leaver destinations and Section 11 support. It also offered guidance for action planning based on careful monitoring and evaluation of the above areas.

(iii)   Football for girls (Welsh Sports Council/Welsh Urban LEA)

The equal opportunities dimension of sport has emerged as a feature of the project as was seen in Chapter 6. In this initiative, over 10 primary schools in the county were involved with the Welsh Sports Council in extending football to girls. A primary school involved in this initiative employed a trainee teacher (female) to take 20 year 5 girls for weekly football sessions.

The idea is to get girls using the playground space and joining in the County's under-13 girls' league.
(Student teacher)

The boys get jealous 'cos we've got our own coach and she teaches us skills...They say 'can we be a girl today?' [giggles]...they won't let us play at dinner time though.
(Year 5 girl in track suit).

7.6   CONCLUSIONS

Various themes and concerns were identified by the project focusing on changing gender cultures in schools, the most important of which are highlighted below.

The language of gender

- Gender issues are now being framed within the new language of schooling arising out of the post-reform era. Some schools have brought gender issues into line with concerns about performance, standards and value-added policies; others have focused on broader based and more inclusive concepts of entitlement and effective citizenship. Thus the language of equal opportunities policy-making has, to some extent, adapted to and become part of the new mainstream culture of schools.

The culture of management

- There appears to be a strong imbalance in the management of LEAs and schools in favour of men. Evidence from the case studies and the surveys suggests that women generally have not made major inroads into the higher levels of educational management and moreover, that many female LEA officers and teachers are intensely aware of the gender bias in policy interests.

- Female teachers' concerns and levels of gender awareness more generally are frequently constrained by the lack of interest (and sometimes hostility) of senior male colleagues and LEA managers.

152

- The male management ethos in some primary schools may have led to the relative neglect of equal opportunities in this sector.

School cultures

- Single-sex schooling was reported as being popular amongst some parents, both for academic performance, and in the case of selective schools, for the variety of extra curricular activities they offered.

- The integration of girls into mixed sixth forms in boys' schools was found to be problematic, if not handled with sensitivity.

- Pupils' perceptions of gender issues, across a range of ages and social groups and localities, were seen as more open and more sensitive to changing cultural expectations and/or changes in the labour market than previously. Thus, girls and young women appeared more confident and positive about their future working lives and opportunities. Boys and young men also seemed aware of gender debates about women's working lives. Nevertheless occupational choices for both sexes remain generally conventional and stereotyped.

Perceived areas of concern

- Concerns about educational inequality have shifted to some extent away from girls' to boys' underachievement and poor behaviour, although this has only recently been seen as a gender (as opposed to disciplinary, minority ethnic or social class) issue. New strategies are thus being developed in some schools to improve male students' performance, in English in particular, and to create a softer, more caring, masculinity.

- Concern nevertheless remains about the conventional nature of young women's educational and work experiences (among all ability groups) and their narrowed occupational choices. Consequently, several initiatives have sought to highlight the broader range of careers and opportunities available - though there has been little training available for this.

- Additional attention has focused on the low achievement or poor behaviour of male or female pupils and students from specific socio-economic or ethnic groups.

- Although they may not be regarded as important, other areas of concern included separation of girls and boys on the register, whether girls should be allowed to wear trousers and whether boys should be allowed to wear earrings.

Practices, policies and initiatives

- Initiatives on equal opportunities have been developed in certain LEAs and schools in England and Wales, although most have been 'in-house' and do not appear to have been widely publicised or discussed. Many of these initiatives specifically address the post-reform context (e.g. OFSTED inspections, value-added policies, monitoring of performance, governor training, women in management), fusing prior considerations premised on social justice with more recent concerns about performance standards.

8   CONCLUSIONS

This report describes a short-term and relatively small scale study of gender equality in British schools over a ten year period (1984-1994). Any findings therefore need to be viewed as indicative of educational or cultural shifts or changes rather than offering any definitive statement on the current educational context. The research had a three-fold aim: to map student performance in terms of gender over a ten year period; to evaluate the impact of government reforms on gender equality in schools; and to ascertain any noticeable changes in student and/or school cultures, and in equal opportunities policy-making. As has been shown, the historical point at which the research was carried out (1994-5) followed, first, a period of equal opportunities activity in education which reached its height in the mid-1980s, in which Local Education Authorities took a major role; and second, a period of educational policy change or reform instigated by central government and operating a mix of tight central control and market forces.

In considering the government reforms of the late 1980s and early 1990s, two clusters of reforms were identified. The first focused on curriculum, assessment and monitoring of performance, namely, the establishment of a National Curriculum, assessment, testing and examinations, monitoring of school performance, and publication of school examinations and results. The second cluster focused on changes to the administration and organisation of schools, namely, shifts from LEA responsibility for the organisation of schools to greater school autonomy and diversity with LMS, open enrolment, increased power of school governing bodies, GMS and CTCs.

Few of the reforms were framed or developed with increased gender equality primarily in mind and hence there is relatively little explicit reference to gender equality in the policy documentation. In order to incorporate equality issues more explicitly into the reforms, therefore, teachers and LEAs developed broader concepts of equal opportunities which fused more readily with government priorities and demands. This led to a wider focus within the research on shifts in perception and interpretation of equal opportunities and/or gender policies and issues.

Rather than providing an analysis of current gender patterns only, one of the main aims of the examination mapping exercise was to show whether patterns of gender difference had changed

155

as a result of the government reforms. However, it should be noted that the limitations of the data, their inadequacy in terms of availability, consistency and comparability, have inhibited the research analysis. In particular, much of the data on examinations cannot easily be disaggregated by gender. In order to compare the changes in the relative performance of male and female students, therefore, the concept of *gender gap* was used to discuss ways in which different patterns of examination entry and performance, curriculum and vocational choice, and entry into the labour market, further and higher education, might be estimated, discussed and planned.

The examination mapping exercise and the school and LEA questionnaire surveys provided trend analyses of patterns of subject choice and qualifications, and of levels of equal opportunities awareness, policies and practices. The value of the case studies was that they offered a more detailed and up-to-date picture of how equality issues were being experienced within schools and at LEA level. What they also showed was the variability in awareness, commitment and experience of equal opportunities policy-making and implementation within and between LEA areas.

The case studies additionally showed the importance of *local* context - for example, history of equal opportunities policy-making, LEA political allegiance, denominational influence - in the development and maintenance of equality issues as an educational priority. This has led to differences in perception of the overall impact of the reforms. In LEA areas with a previous longstanding commitment to equal opportunities, gender was perceived as having shifted *down* the policy agenda post-1988, as the LEA lost its powers to influence and coordinate policies in schools. In contrast, small shifts *upwards* were identified by schools and LEAs which, for the first time, have been compelled by procedures arising out of the reforms, to address gender issues in their reporting and evaluation procedures.

8.1   MAIN FINDINGS

Subject entry and performance

- Gender differences in performance are evident at the earliest stages of schooling, and vary according to subject and age. From SATs pilot schemes, boys, in particular, appear to be underachieving in English at KS1 and KS2.

156

- There has been a considerable increase overall in entry into GCSE with female students in particular increasing their take-up across the full range of subjects.

- Female students have improved their performance markedly (in relation to entry) for GCSE in Mathematics and Science in particular, whereas male students have not shown similar improvements in their examination performance, achieving relatively less well in English, the Arts, Humanities and Modern Foreign Languages.

- For GCSE, girls' schools generally achieve exceptionally good results.

- At A-level, pronounced gender differences in subject choice and entry emerge with female students failing to close the traditional gender gap favouring male students in Mathematics and Science. However, male students are closing the gender gap in favour of female students in the Humanities subjects.

- Female A-level students have improved their performance in almost all subjects, often where they are in the minority. They are also gaining a larger share of high grades in most subjects.

- The ten-year period has seen a considerable rise in achievement of compulsory and post-compulsory qualifications, particularly by young women.

- In terms of vocational qualifications, the gender gap remains favourable to young men, particularly for certain minority ethnic groups. Nevertheless, young women appear to have a better record of course completion.

- Sex stereotyping in the selection of vocational courses remains a continuing feature of vocational education with young men and women choosing to study for different occupational qualifications.

- Assessment data (such as SATs, GCSE and A-level) which require a breakdown according to gender, have raised awareness of gender issues. The value of such data is illustrated by the research findings. A more sophisticated gender analysis requires regular, routine data collection, disaggregated by sex by the relevant agencies viz.

OFSTED, SCAA, DFEE, NCVQ. If collected on an annual basis, such data would also provide valuable insights into the inter-relationship between male and female achievement patterns and social class, ethnicity, bilingualism and special educational needs.

Equal opportunities policy-making

- Wide variation exists regarding the awareness and application of gender equality, interpretation of equal opportunities and student performance trends, and in prioritisation of equality issues.

- The majority of LEAs and schools have policies on equal opportunities, either with gender as a specific focus or as one of a number equality themes. Significantly, the majority of schools developed equal opportunities policies after 1989.

- The main impetus for the development of equal opportunities policies and practices has come from LEAs and headteachers in the case of primary schools, and from LEAs, headteachers, committed teachers and TVEI in the case of secondary schools. In contrast, there has been little interest forthcoming from governors or parents and the impact of OFSTED has been uneven.

- Fewer primary than secondary schools had equal opportunities policies in place. Primary schools can also have a management culture that discourages wider take-up of equal opportunities issues. One reason for this is that primary schools view equal opportunities as integrated into their practice rather than as a discrete priority.

- There appears to be no shared characteristic of grant maintained schools; therefore no single approach to equal opportunities policy-making could be identified. Other factors seemed as important as grant maintained status e.g. selective admissions policy, single sex/coeducational provision, and LMS.

- At LEA level, equal opportunities practice is generally low key with few specific or specialist posts for gender and little evidence that gender equality constitutes a priority.

- A proportion of LEAs and schools involved in the research claimed that equal opportunities has become a higher priority as a result of specific reforms, though a substantial minority came to the opposite conclusion.

- Different perceptions emerged (from LEAs as opposed to schools) about the extent of LEA provision of equal opportunities training and other services, for schools. LEAs claimed to be providing more on equal opportunities than schools described themselves as receiving. In particular, schools mentioned a lack of LEA support for monitoring and in-service training. These different perceptions are likely to have been caused by the changed relationship between schools and LEAs as a result of the introduction of LMS.

Impact of specific reforms

- Changes to the curriculum, assessment and system of examination, monitoring of male and female performance and increased data collection were all perceived to have had a largely positive effect on gender equality in schools. The introduction of GCSE, the National Curriculum, TVEI and OFSTED inspections were seen as particularly important in raising the profile of gender equality.

- Perceptions of the impact of the reforms relating to the organisation of schools were less positive in relation to gender equality, particularly by LEAs. The impact on equal opportunities of the introduction of LMS, the sharp reduction in LEA influence and the creation of grant maintained status drew the most criticism.

Changing gender cultures

- The language of equal opportunities has shifted to address post-reform priorities, placing greater emphasis on standards, performance, rights and responsibility and rather less on increasing social justice.

- The management of schools and LEAs appears overwhelmingly male with women in general failing to reach the higher levels of power and decision-making. This, it has been claimed, has led to a lack of sensitivity and/or urgency about promoting greater gender equality; and concern among women teachers about their lack of status and professional reputation.

- In contrast, pupils and students appear less stereotyped in their view of gender relations. Perceptions of gender issues across the spectrum of ages, social groups, achievement ranges and localities, are more sensitive to changing cultural and labour market expectations about the nature of men's and women's lives and work.

- Perceived areas of concern include girls' narrowed educational and work aspirations, the underachievement and poor behaviour of boys, and the need to focus equality policies on targeted under-achieving groups of girls and boys e.g. working class boys, Asian girls.

- A number of initiatives on equal opportunities have been developed by schools and LEAs, most of which specifically address the priorities of the post-reform period, but which also contain a firm commitment to increased social justice.

8.2   GENERAL POLICY IMPLICATIONS

- The introduction of *comprehensive and uniform monitoring of achievement* levels by gender (as well as for other social categories) has revealed the importance of such measures in identifying educational and occupational targets and patterns for males and females. This suggests that such monitoring of national targets is continued and related to specific equality targets for schools, LEAs and other educational agencies.

- The examination mapping exercise undertaken for the project was inhibited by the limitations and inadequacies of available data. In particular, much of the data on examinations, school leaver qualifications, and vocational course awards are not disaggregated by sex. This study therefore, draws attention to the need for an effective national system of data collection of examination performance and course awards data according to gender, using consistent base-lines and age cohort data.

- The quality of the information gained from the case studies and, in particular, the focus on how gender issues are *experienced* by different individuals and groups has confirmed the importance of such forms of *focused qualitative research* in understanding specific processes of gender difference in schools and in education more generally.

- The analysis of performance trends has identified a *number of concerns*:

  - the continuing narrowed aspirations of girls and young women when selecting subject options and future occupational possibilities, despite their improved performance, relative to boys, in examinations;
  - the relative underachievement of boys and young men in English, Languages and the Humanities in schooling up to KS4;
  - the relative failure of young women to take up Mathematics and the Sciences post-16 and also to opt for sex-stereotyped subjects;
  - the resolutely sex-stereotyped nature of vocational educational choices and qualifications for both young women and young men;
  - male over-representation in LEA and school management hierarchies which can provide obstacles to the development of strategies to reduce gender inequality and discrimination;
  - the recent re-introduction (post-Dearing) of greater choice at KS3 onwards and in vocational education might lead to higher levels of sex-stereotyping in subject choice for students of both sexes.

- The positive identification of *strong central direction* with increased gender awareness - e.g. OFSTED equal opportunities criteria or TVEI equal opportunities requirements - suggests that equality initiatives that demand targets and accountability are likely to be more effective than those mainly dependent on individual commitment or voluntary effort. This suggests that national gender targets could usefully be developed by relevant agencies (e.g. SCAA, DFEE, OFSTED, NCVQ and awarding bodies) and used as a yardstick for systematic monitoring of equal opportunities.

- *Gaps in equal opportunities support* are noticeable despite increased development of equal opportunities policies etc. These include lack of:

  - governor training and classroom-focused INSET;
  - awareness and involvement of parents and parent-governors;
  - awareness among headteachers and classroom teachers (particularly at primary level), of the range of policy and curriculum strategies available;
  - coordinated specialist resource centres and libraries; and
  - coordinated equal opportunities networks and advisory expertise.

161

● The patterns of subject choice and examination performance in vocational education identified by the project suggest the importance of *monitoring and evaluating the new framework of vocational qualifications* in terms of gender, if previous outdated sex-typed work patterns are to be challenged and eradicated.

8.3   CONCLUDING POINTS

Far from the gloomy predictions of some regarding the nature of gender in/equality in schools and LEAs in England and Wales in the mid-1990s, the research revealed a mixed picture of beneficial procedures and policies arising from some of the reforms, pockets of thoughtful and knowledgeable practice from committed individuals and groups but overall, no infrastructure for the delivery of equal opportunities on a wider and more systematic basis.

Cultural, demographic and labour market changes have clearly influenced the way students and teachers think about the schooling of girls and boys such that few now consider girls' education to be less important. In fact high-scoring female students are proving attractive to schools in the competitive climate of the 1990s, and it is poorly behaved and low achieving boys who appear to be the subjects of greatest concern.

This should not lead policy-makers and practitioners into the error of concluding that boys are now the educationally disadvantaged sex. Indeed, male 'underachievement' tends to disappear after 16, when many young men reassert their advantage over young women, for example, at A-level, in vocational qualifications, in higher education and in the labour market. Nevertheless some boys and young men appear particularly disadvantaged, not necessarily because of poor schooling, but because of the forms of masculinity they adopt and because of the collapse of traditional forms of male work available to their fathers. It is then often left to schools to pick up the pieces and it has been clear, as has been noted in this report, that schools are attempting to address what might be regarded as a 'moral panic' about the education of boys in constructive and important ways.

However, there are wide areas that it has not been possible for the project to address: for example, the variable and often large, differences between girls' and boys' experiences in the variety of schools of the post-reform period; the impact of social class and minority ethnic origin on gender differences in academic and vocational performance; the extent and depth of understanding and perception of gender issues in schools (including special schools) in England and Wales; and the forms of curriculum and policy support most likely to support the achievement of increased gender equality in schools and more widely.

If the shifts towards greater gender equality identified by the project are to continue, efforts need to be made to explore those issues that were not addressed by the project (as above), to create a sound infrastructure for the delivery of equal educational opportunities, and to build upon the commitment of the many involved in education to providing genuinely better opportunities for future generations of female and male citizens, as parents and as workers.

163

APPENDIX A   PROJECT METHODOLOGY

This chapter includes information about aspects of the research which, for reasons of brevity and consistency of discussion, has not been included elsewhere in the report.

The first section considers debates concerning the methodology adopted for the performance mapping exercise (the findings of which are reported in Chapters 3 and 4) and in particular the use of the concept of the 'gender gap'. The second section focuses on the questionnaire surveys, and in particular, how problems concerning the initial low response rate were addressed. And the final section focuses on the use of a Research Contract as a basis of agreement between the case study LEAs and schools, and the project team.

A.1   ASSESSING GENDER PERFORMANCE[1]

This section is concerned with the development of a methodology for monitoring gender equality over time, which shows how each and every gender gap has changed (or not) over the last ten years. There may well be arguments about whether any gap, any group of gaps or all gaps should (or should not) be zero. The view is taken here that genuine equality of opportunity need not, in all cases, lead to a zero gap, especially in the post-16 arena where choice plays such a major part in forming the data.

The years featured

For purposes of mapping trends four 'snapshot' years at equally-spaced intervals were selected: 1985, 1988, 1991 and 1994.

In 1985 the academic provision for Year 11 students was either through GCE O-levels or through the CSE, although by that time there was a significant number of joint examinations provided by consortia of GCE and CSE boards. The corresponding Year 13 provision was via the GCE-level.

In 1988 the GCSE became the regular pathway for Year 11 students. As well as academic syllabuses there was a variety of vocationally-related schemes. For all subjects bar Mathematics,

---

[1]   Prepared for the Project Team by Charles Newbould, Oxford and Cambridge Schools Examination Board.

a coursework element was compulsory and in some cases comprised the complete assessment. The GCE-level remained structurally unchanged.

By 1991 GCSE coursework regulations had spread to include Mathematics and there had been a considerable growth of double award (two grades the same) and dual award (two potentially different grades) syllabuses. The A-level syllabuses had been revised to accommodate the changes in prior study brought about by the GCSE and had been supplemented by the AS provision.

By 1994 the National Curriculum orders in English, Mathematics and Science were in place in England and Wales for the GCSE, with associated restrictions in coursework provision and a re-introduction of all-examination possibilities. 'Tiering' (a system whereby candidates are given different tasks according to perceived capability) became compulsory in these subject areas. There had also been a considerable decline in the Mode 3 (100 per cent coursework) provision as a result of the phasing out of 100 per cent coursework schemes. A new grade (Starred A) was added to the top of the scale. There had been some change in the A-level provision as a result of the growth of modular schemes but the introduction of GNVQ had also seen a re-direction of some of the cohort away from the 'academic' pathway.

Focus on students

The study mapping has two key variables: *curriculum choice* and the *attainment of qualifications*. Whilst each of these would appear perfectly straightforward, this is far from the case. In the first place, curricular choice is partly governed by policies (at the national, local or institutional level), partly by resources (the availability of sufficient and suitably trained staff and an appropriate array of facilities), partly by future (career) prospects and partly by student preferences. Thus, for example, growth in the study of Science pre-16 and decline in the study of Science post-16 are almost certainly unrelated - the first is largely attributable to policy, the second to preferences and, to a degree, declining prospects (Tarsh et al. 1994).

Furthermore curriculum choice, whilst normally made at key points within the process of education and training, is not solely confined to these times. Students (sometimes in large numbers - Audit Commission 1993) drop out of courses, change from one subject to another or from one qualification target to another (for example, the provision of both A-level and AS routes within a scheme enables students to delay choices about qualification targets until well into a course). In particular, the manifestations of choice evident at the conclusion of courses, as measured by submission for assessment, neither totally reflect those at the beginning of courses nor, indeed (see below), necessarily reflect course completion[2].

The acquisition of qualifications has, for most students in recent times, been largely concurrent: that is, each student has followed a number of courses in parallel, has submitted for examination/assessment for all of these at the end of each course (that is, at the same time) and has received a set of results. Underlying this, however, has been a practice, common in some schools and some subjects, of accelerating study in one or two areas in order to start some pupils on more advanced courses early. Consequently the acquisition of qualifications has been staggered rather than concurrent. In contrast it has also become common practice for students to resubmit for assessment in cases where results in critical subjects fall below target grades which might affect future access to forms of Higher Education. Both of these circumstances indicate correlation between occurrence and ability but they are otherwise quite different.

An additional complication has arisen in recent years with the growth of assessment schemes supporting modular courses. Here the student can, in a way not possible with a terminal assessment regime (as above), control the point at which a qualification is sought or indeed whether a failing performance is ever registered.

The two foci are, of course, connected. Whilst it is self-evident that there can be no qualification data without a (prior) curriculum choice, it is far from self-evident what the other connections are. It is becoming increasingly obvious, however, that perceptions of difficulty (in achieving a given qualification) are impacting on choice - both in terms of course provision and in students' own choices from amongst those courses offered.

As well as these problems, there are issues related to the collection and presentation of data which have an impact on the capacity to quantify choice and qualifications and hence, insofar as these issues are time-related, to monitor change in the system. These are explored below.

---

[2]   A note of the scale of absentees: those entering public examinations and receiving no result, either through total or partial absence.

The limitations of data

The strategy adopted for the project has been, to a large extent, dictated by the nature of the available data. Whilst it is not possible to apply a cause and effect model to assess the effect on choice and qualifications of the various educational reforms, it is reasonable to expect that the impact of any particular reform would be time-related, even if by no means instantaneous. As such the ideal cohort of students for monitoring purposes would be those whose common links are the courses of study which they have shared (the *study* cohort). No data sources we have been able to access, however, are based on this unit.

What data are available are based on one of three other cohort groupings. The first, which has become more dominant in recent years in publications from central government, is an *age* cohort. Usually the data relate to events up to and including a particular date (usually 31 August) in a particular year (which ensures all in the cohort have thereby attained a significant age - 7, 11, 14, 16 and 18 being the usual markers). Those whose cohort of study is in advance of their age may well not have their curricular choices and qualification successes included in the data but those who are 'out of phase' in the other direction, or who acquire further (relevant) qualifications at some later date, will either be excluded from the data or will appear less capable than they are.

In earlier government publications the emphasis was on the cohort of (school) *leavers*. Here students from different age cohorts and those from different study cohorts were mixed together in the same tabulations. Whilst it can be argued that in a situation of 'stable state' the mix could be seen as a reasonable proxy for an age cohort (for example, those staying on through the sixth form having very similar characteristics to those planning to stay on 'now') once cohorts change markedly in size (see later for details), or when major reforms are introduced, this approximation can no longer hold.

Many publications relating to subject-specific (or syllabus-specific) qualifications (be they of attempt or of success) use a third cohort: the point at which eligibility for the *qualification* has been assessed. In many ways this best approximates to the study cohort because it is commonly the case that courses leading to the same qualification are of the same length and that students enter for examinations or submit work for assessment at the end of the course. Clearly, however, data from students pursuing a course of study of the 'normal length' are added to by those accelerating their study and those (part-time students, possibly) taking longer. There is inevitably, therefore, a mix of ages within a qualification cohort.

These cohorts have a property which is quite distinct from the other ones and which is thus likely to be less familiar to most readers: the unit of counting is *not* that of a student. If, for example, a student seeks qualifications in four different subject areas then (s)he appears four times in the cohort - once for each 'entry'. Thus data from this source contains a number of particular ability-related biases. For example, the more able one is the more likely it is that one gains more, as well as better, qualifications. On the other hand, in some schools, the more able one is the more likely it is that qualifications will be phased and thus some successes will appear in one dataset and some in another. As some of these attainments occur in the autumn/winter examination sessions, which are invariably excluded from such publications, the cohort may appear less successful than the persons in it actually are.

Issues of availability

Whilst 1985, 1988, 1991 and 1994 have been chosen as the four 'snapshot' years, it has not always been possible to identify data from those years, especially when using information from government departments. It has been possible, however, to use data from examination board sources, based on qualification cohorts, which are reasonably consistent between the years both in form and in groupings.

It is also necessary to register what significant data are not available. Despite repeated attempts by staff of the National Council for Vocational Qualifications to obtain data about vocational qualifications (past and present), it has not been possible to include any such data in the study, beyond that which is summarised in Department of Education and Science (DES) and Department of Education publications. The magnitude of this omission cannot be estimated and thus its significance cannot be judged. Of particular note are the following:

- achievements of vocational and/or pre-vocational qualifications by KS4 students are absent;

- achievements of vocational and/or pre-vocational qualifications by full-time students in post-16 education and training are absent;

- all present-day vocational qualifications are modular in construction which means that, as in the case of modular GCE qualifications, submission for (final) assessment significantly under-represents contemporary curricular participation;

- NVQs are ungraded; and

- the equivalence of A-level GCE and GNVQ qualifications is no more than a hypothesis at present (SCAA is currently investigating this relationship).

Issues of base

The different data sources use an array of geographical bases. Some data relate to England only, some to England and Wales, some to the UK, some either exclude the whole of Scotland or just include those cases where non-Scottish qualifications are used. For some purposes, a UK base includes data from students abroad - certain forces' schools and international establishments are included because they follow a wholly 'English' curriculum.

Whilst the Welsh Office publish some information about samples of leavers in that country they do *not* publish examination statistics for students in Welsh schools - they replicate the statistics for the Welsh Joint Education Committee, which include performances of some students in England and exclude those of many in Wales. Consequently both England and Wales are included within the one set of analyses presented in what follows.

Changes in cohort sizes

There have been major changes in the size and sometimes the composition of these various cohorts over the last few years. These are briefly described below and the 16 year-old and 18 year-old cohorts over the last ten years are shown in Table 9.1.

It is clear that, over the period as a whole, there has been a marked decline in the size of school intakes, which is only now beginning to reverse. Whilst it is difficult to quantify the extent to which this decline has affected course provision overall, it seems unlikely that it has had no effect on either provision or on the resources within an institution (for example, a fall in the level of capitation may have immediately led to rises in the threshold of uneconomic teaching groups and thus to the reduction in the breadth of course provision).

Table A.1   **Cohort size 1984-1994** [1]

Number of 15 year olds		Number of 17 year olds	
Year	Number[2]	Year	Number[2]
1984	740.5	1984	778.8
1985	731.5	1985	760.7
1986	711.4	1986	744.1
1987	721.3	1987	734.9
1988	672.9	1988	715.1
1989	630.2	1989	724.2
1990	595.5	1990	676.4
1991	572.8	1991	634.5
1992	553.3	1992	602.2
1993	534.5	1993	579.4
1994	549.0	1994	556.7

[1]   Numbers for 1984-1993 actual, 1994 projected

[2]   Number in thousands

Source: Office of Population Censuses and Surveys, Government Actuary's Department

At a more basic level marked reductions in student numbers have inevitably led to lower absolute numbers appearing in official statistics, regardless of any relative changes which may have taken place.

The impact on the other cohorts, although less marked, is equally significant. Leavers' cohorts, being comprised of data from three or more age cohorts, were bound to reflect those elements differently as each earlier (age) cohort was actually larger.

Provision of qualifications, in part, reflects market forces. For example, policy moves towards 'Science for All' have limited the range of choice between different syllabuses in the separate sciences of Biology, Chemistry and Physics and have largely killed off a number of minority sciences (with titles such as Rural, Electronics, Geology, Astronomy). Provision also reflects cohort size. If, for example, a qualification is offered so long as it attracts at least 500 entries per annum, then it will disappear if the cohort size reduces, unless it suddenly becomes relatively more popular. Once lost it would be most unlikely to return simply because a future age cohort was larger than the present one. Consequently the characteristics of the qualifications cohort might change even if its overall size does not.

For the most part published data do not indicate the proportion of age cohorts present in the statistics reported for either leavers' or qualifications' cohorts. As is indicated above, it is inevitable that over time the proportions of age groups within the leavers' data change. What is not known is the extent to which this is, or is not, true about qualification cohorts. What is known, however, is that in all years the numbers of students in a qualification cohort who are not in the targeted age cohort constitute a significant minority (estimated to be of the order of 20 per cent or more - see below).

Whilst some educational reforms relate specifically to course provision or the balance of an overall course, others relate to destinations. The rate of staying-on after the end of compulsory schooling can be, and has been, affected by adjustments in the range and character of the destinations of the students or by the 'knock-on' effect of changes earlier in the system. Thus, for example, whilst it can be argued that changes in the two key variables within Key Stage 4 are now broadly circumscribed by policy, the impact on both future decisions (to stay on) and choices (what track to join and what to study) is unlikely to be neutral, regardless of any policy directives aimed specifically at that target group.

This may be exemplified by the fact that over the period under study the take-up of GCE qualifications (A-and AS-level) has grown markedly in absolute terms, despite the continued decline in the numbers of students falling within the (age-related) target group.

Thus, for purposes of comparison, it was necessary to identify some means of being able to set changes in the absolute numbers choosing courses of study, and/or gaining qualifications as a result, against the backcloth of declining numbers in the target groups for whom the courses and qualifications are designed. The methods for doing this, and the assumptions which have been made, are described below.

Indexing

For reasons articulated above, it is clear that the presentation of data in the form of absolute numbers would not be very helpful. It would be no more helpful, however, simply to report qualification successes as proportions of (subject) choice. A strong case exists for the creation of one, or more, index(es) to enable comparison across time to be made.

This, for the many reasons described above, is not easy. Thus, an attempt has been made to estimate, wherever possible, the figures which would apply to the age cohort, were such statistics available across the years of study.

The following describes the derivation of indices which are used later to represent the entries to, and successes from, the public examining system (GCSE, GCE and formerly CSE).

Indexing 16+ examinations

As was indicated above, no published data relate to study cohorts and only some recent (DfE) data relate to age cohorts. Examination data, however, come from the qualification cohort (all those submitting for (final) assessment in a given session). Qualification cohorts suffer three limitations as proxies: they include students from widely differing age cohorts; they exclude data from the target age cohort because some students enter examinations out of phase; and they use syllabus entry and not the student as the unit of counting.

So, for example in 1991, 657,089 entered for a GCSE examination with the title English. The best estimate is that 555,190 people were born between 1/9/74 and 31/8/75 and were still alive on 31/8/90. DES sources suggest that 521,150 of these (94 per cent) had entered one or more GCSE examinations by the summer of 1991. So, even if every single one had entered for an English examination in 1991, there were still at least as many as 135,939 examination entries (21 per cent of the total) outside the age cohort. Other published sources indicate (albeit for 1993 and not 1991) that the Year 11 cohort (the target age cohort for GCSE) has by age 16 totalled about 80 per cent of all GCSE entries in the target year. Thus, on these data anyway, entries to English (the subject attracting the largest single entry) show the same balance (in and out of target age cohort) as the entries for all subjects combined.

It is necessary, of course, to consider data for male and female students separately, but the official statistics do not provide the relevant breakdowns in all years. It is known, however, that in 1991 altogether 4,947,502 entries for GCSE examinations were received (7.5 times the number of entries to English). It is also known that 49 per cent of these came from males and that a very similar proportion of the English entry came from male students. It can thus be concluded that it is reasonably safe to adopt the entries to English as the gender baselines[3].

All other figures for 1991, therefore, are divided by the number of males or females entering English and, to avoid decimal fractions, multiplied by 100 and rounded. So, for example, the index for females entering History is 34.

There are two immediate benefits of an index such as this:

i)   It can be used without amendment for both *choice*, as manifest by application for an examination result, and for *qualification*, as manifest by examination grade reached.

ii)   It is additive, in the sense that summing the choice indices across all subjects gives an estimate of the average number of subjects studied, or summing across all A-C indices, for example, estimates the average number of Grades A-C achieved nationally.

Indexing A-level examinations

As far as choice and performance post-16 are concerned, whilst the same requirements of an index are desired the same procedure does not make sense. That adopted for the GCSE data in effect assumes that, regardless of different age-cohort mixes in the qualifications cohort, a reasonable working assumption is that if a candidate takes only one GCSE then it is almost certain to be in English. In the GCE, however, where most students enter three A-levels, there is no core subject. The alternative derivation is described below, again using 1991 for illustrative purposes.

Official sources indicate that in 1991 the target age cohort contained 637,800, of which 149,380 (23 per cent) had taken one or more GCE examination by that date. GCE A-level entries (AS figures, being small, are disregarded in what follows) totalled 699,029. As this is as much as 4.7 times the number in the target age cohort having entered the GCE, it is clear that a significant proportion of the entry came from outside that group. Calculation based on 1993 data

---

[3]   A validation study has been carried out on data from 1993, which although not one of the target years in this research, has publications for both the qualification cohorts for GCSE and GCE and the Year 11 and Year 13 age-based cohorts.

(when, to meet the requirements of the *Parents' Charter*, the national data were merged for the first time) indicate that 70 per cent of the national GCE entry came from the target age cohort.

On this basis it can be estimated that 489,320 entries came from the target age cohort, which yields a much more realistic estimate of an average of 3.3 entries per person (whilst the norm is three A-levels, over 50,000 entries to General Studies are mostly beyond the norm). The GCE index thus uses the 70 per cent multiplier to estimate the proportion in Year 13 and then relates the outcome to the number of males/females in the age cohort known to have taken at least one GCE. Two examples follow.

Overall there were 75,640 females in Year 13 who entered one or more GCEs in 1991. In A-level Physics there were 9,773 entries and so the *choice* index is calculated as 9. There were 34,999 females achieving a grade (A-E) in A-level English Literature, so that particular *qualification* index was 32.

The assumptions underlying this derivation are, it is recognised, weaker than those made in the GCSE case. There are, for example, certain GCE subjects which are particularly (and hence differentially) attractive to out-of-age students. For example, the number of younger students entering Mathematics is known to be greater than average, as is the number of older students studying Art. What is hoped, however, is that despite these obvious weaknesses trends across time and between the sexes can still be explored via the one indexing procedure.

Finally it should be noted that in both contexts (GCSE and GCE) there is more than one possible qualifications index (there is, in theory, one for each grade on the scale) and the gender gap may be different in the different cases. This report confines itself to reporting those grade points which are deemed the most significant to users.

Derivation of the gender gap[4]

This sub-section centres its attention on the way in which the differential gender performances are calculated. Since, clearly, straightforward numbers can be misleading, as mentioned previously, a method needs to be devised which shows these differentials in an unbiased way.

---

[4] This section prepared for the Project Team by Elizabeth Gray, Oxford and Cambridge Schools Examination Board.

Additionally, it is important to quantify any changes in this performance gap over time in order to identify any trends.

There are various ways in which this can be done, but for a number of reasons the method described below was chosen and has been used throughout the analysis of examination performances at GCSE and A-level.

Ratio rather than difference in method of determining gender gaps has the advantage in that it can reduce to a single figure for each year and hence be illustrated by a single line. The technique described here is based on a ratio such that the relative proportions of males to females are found for entry and performance. The sign of the measure shows the gender which predominates. For Science in 1988, the performance index for males was 157, for females 141; this is a ratio of 157:141. It is important to remember that the starting point is 100 for each gender, thus the ratio does not mean that the Year 11 population is divided 157:141 because that would take no account of the *relative* proportions of males to females in the population. This is not a trivial point, and is analogous to the relationship between entry and performance identified by expectations.

Thus, from the entry figures, one would expect that $157/(157+141)$, or 52.7 per cent of the performance figures, would be ascribed to males, and 47.3 per cent to females. In fact, from the performance numbers of 71 and 61, the percentages are 53.8 per cent and 46.2 per cent. Therefore, girls are still under-represented at the higher grades than their entry indices would indicate. Condensing this argument, if one took the entry gender gap, i.e. $(157-141)/(157+141)$, and the performance gender gap, in this case $(71-61)/(71+61)$, and subtracted them, then a single indicator, here (5.37-7.6) or -2.23, would serve to show the equal representation (or otherwise) of the genders in the performance figures. Here the gap is wider for performance than entry, thus negative for girls. The closer to zero, the more equivalent the proportion of genders in the performance data, given the proportion at entry.

More formally, the approach adopted for this report quantifies the gender gap as shown below:-

$$G = \frac{M - F}{M + F} * 100.0$$

G = gender gap of entry (or performance)

M = male entry (or performance) index

F = female entry (or performance) index

Perhaps of more direct application is that the two gender gaps of entry and performance can be combined by subtracting GP, the gender gap of performance, from GE, the gender gap of entry. This leaves a single measure which, in sign and magnitude, suffices to indicate both the gender which, given its entry, shows best and, over time, whether the difference between male and female performances is increasing, decreasing or remaining the same.

The gender gap is graphically illustrated in Chapters 3 and 4 for most major subject areas; there are, however, one or two general points to be made about their interpretation, though they are fairly self evident:

i)   G, as defined, will be zero if the male index is equal to the female index.

ii)   G, as defined, will be positive if the male index is greater than the female index, negative if less.

iii)   Given the above, if (GE-GP) is negative, then males have a better than expected performance; if (GE-GP) is positive, then females dominate the performance figures once allowance has been made for the size of entry.

iv)   The magnitude of (GE-GP) is a measure of the percentage difference between expected and actual performance and may be used to define trends.

The data from which the histograms and graphs in Chapters 3 and 4 were drawn are included as Appendix B.

Focus on schools

For the last three years the provisions of the *Parent's Charter* have required that, on an annual basis, performance tables are published. These list, for each school, certain variables which provide performance indicators (based on GCSE results for Year 11 pupils) for the students within the school, and other variables which provide contextual information about the institution itself. Starting with 1993 these data have been made available by the DfE in computer-readable form. It is through these data that the project has been able to take a snapshot, using the 1994 data, specifically to address one question: is there any evidence that the gender balance of the school (mixed, male only, female only) has any impact on the quality of the performances produced?

The study of this issue has been confined to Key Stage 4 for several reasons, some pragmatic, some theoretical. In most areas (from nursery through to higher education) institutions are co-educational, even if, as is still the case with a number of selective schools in particular, this is confined to Years 12 and 13. Likewise, teaching groups are not segregated, although student choices may make them so. It is the case, however, that post-16 there is very little single-sex schooling and it is nearly always because the institution is for younger pupils.

It is, of course, true that selective schools are more likely to be single-sex than comprehensive schools, so there is an unavoidable interaction effect. Indeed it could be argued that a single-sex comprehensive school is, by that very designation, atypical of the broader class. The project analyses explore whether differences in performance between the three types of gender organisation reveal any kind of pattern which replicates across the different types of institutions.

It should also be noted that, as in all secondary data analysis, the researcher is limited by the quality or range of data provided. The performance tables give overall performance indicators (in particular the proportion of the age cohort gaining five or more Grades A-C) and not ones broken down by gender. Thus only in single-sex schools can one confidently assign the value of the indicator to females or to males, as appropriate, and not in the great majority of (co-educational) cases, where even the relative numbers of males to females is not recorded.

A.2   SURVEYS OF LEAS, PRIMARY AND SECONDARY SCHOOLS

This section focuses on the administration and distribution of the questionnaires and the attendant problems, and should be seen as providing additional information to that in Chapter 1.

In the absence of a database covering the whole range of schools in England and Wales, a national sampling frame was drawn up by the Schools Government Publishing Company based upon data for maintained schools in England and Wales for 1993-94. We decided to exclude from the sampling frame all special schools and sixth form colleges deemed further education; and there were a number of difficulties with the definitions of primary and secondary schools, especially in terms of middle schools. The sampling frame was not stratified or structured in terms of region, locality or type of school. On the basis of the information given, that there were 20,168 such primary schools in England and Wales, they drew a 1 in 20 random sample from 18,170 primary (including separate infant and junior) and middle (deemed primary) schools

177

(county, voluntary and GM) in England and 1698 primary LEA-controlled schools in Wales (including GMS, voluntary and county). There were 4,309 secondary schools in England and Wales and a 1 in 4 random sample was drawn from amongst 3,426 secondary maintained schools in England (including county, voluntary, middle deemed secondary and sixth form colleges), 233 secondary LEA-controlled schools in Wales and 650 GM schools in England and Wales. All 15 CTCs existing in 1993-4 were also drawn.

The LEA questionnaire was distributed to all LEAs in England (112) and Wales (8), 120 in total.

Table A.2   **Details of the three postal survey samples**

	Total population	Achieved sample	No. of responses	Percentage responses
Primary Schools				
England	18,170	943	357	38
GM England and Wales	300	18	2	11
Wales	1,698	85	31	36
Total	20,168	1,046	390	
Secondary Schools				
England	3,426	701	188	27
GM England and Wales	650	155	26	17
Wales	233	55	12	21
CTC[1]	[2]	15	9	60
Total	4,309	926	235	
LEAs				
England	112	112	49	44
Wales	8	8	3	38

[1]   All CTCs were surveyed, as were all LEAs in England and Wales

[2]   The 15 CTCs are included in the overall figure for England of 3426

The Welsh questionnaires (151) were translated into Welsh before being distributed to 58 secondary schools including 3 grant-maintained, 85 primary schools (no GM) and 8 LEAs.

In late August 1994, questionnaires were sent in England to:

961   primary schools, (including 943 LEA and 18 Grant maintained schools);

868   secondary schools (including all (15) CTCs and 701 LEA Secondary schools and 152 Grant Maintained Schools);

112   LEAs;

1941   questionnaires for England only.

The response rate by end of September was less than 30 per cent overall, so a follow-up letter was sent (in October and November) requesting that respondents either return the questionnaire that they had already received or telephone for a duplicate to be sent. This was accompanied again with a supporting letter from the Equal Opportunities Commission. In fact, follow-up letters in England were sent to:

685   primary schools (with an EOC statement)

689   secondary schools (with an EOC statement)

84   LEA letters (with an EOC statement)

1458   letters in total.

In the event, the following response rate was achieved to the three questionnaires in England; a total of 49 replies from the 112 LEAs, making an LEA response rate of 44 per cent; a total of 359 replies from 961 primary schools, providing a primary school response rate of 38 per cent; and a total of 223 replies from 868 secondary schools, providing a secondary school response rate of 26 per cent.

Three replies was received from the Welsh LEAs (37.5 per cent). In the case of the Welsh primary schools, 31 responses were received from a sample of 85 - a response rate of 36 per cent; in the case of the Welsh secondary schools, 12 replies were received - a response rate of 21 per cent.

Over a hundred telephone calls were received which echoed the points made by those teachers and LEA officers who took the time to send a letter or a note explaining why they were not participating. Fifty written refusals were received, the vast majority of which were from secondary schools. The telephone calls and written responses provide a ready source of data and

179

suggested some reasons for the response rate. The fact that so many non-participants actively sought to contact the project suggests the relative importance of the research but perhaps more so the difficulties educational professionals are experiencing currently. As one senior secondary school teacher with an interest and brief to look at equal opportunities said:

> *We have a working group which is due to meet for the first time next Thursday when we will address the Secondary Schools Survey and start collating information....I hope that this will be acceptable to you as the survey will be useful to 'kick start' our venture here and to aid us in looking at EO 'Post-OFSTED'.*

Non-participants expressed a wide range of viewpoints on why they were not able to complete the questionnaire, many of which concerned the timing and appropriateness of the study. It also became clear that a number of questionnaires never reached their intended destinations, and were lost somewhere between the university's post system, the Royal Mail and the various schools' mail rooms. Similarly, some schools had changed names, addresses, structure or simply ceased to exist between the identification of the sample and the administration of the survey. Some sixth-form colleges claimed that the questionnaire had no direct relevance for them or their pupils.

However, almost all non-participants pointed out that, it was the pressures on their time and resources that were the reasons for their inability to complete the questionnaire. As one primary school headteacher with responsibility for Equal Opportunities said:

> *I did not have time to complete the original questionnaire. I started but it became too involved and ceased to be a priority...If you wish you can send another questionnaire but I'm afraid it will not be at the top of my list of priorities.*

Particular reasons were given for the pressure on time, for example, related to preparing for, undergoing or responding to OFSTED inspections, integrating new staff or illness of the person responsible for equal opportunities. The problem of limited time and competing needs led, perhaps inevitably, to the question of incentives - a point raised by a number of those contacting the project. As one secondary headteacher wrote:

In view of under-funding and consequent pressure on time and resources we are no longer prepared to provide such information free of charge. We will undertake to complete the survey upon payment of £50.00 for the teacher and clerical time involved. Please inform us if you wish to proceed on this basis.

Another reason for the relatively disappointing response rate may have related to, ironically, the social and educational changes which provided the main focus of the project. The changes in the education sector have also led to a dramatic increase in the amount of research on schools, a point made by a number of non-respondents. As another primary Headteacher commented:

Headteachers, particularly the primary headteacher,…simply does not have the time to be filling in the deluge of questionnaires which repeatedly fall through the letter box. I have made it my policy to only fill in questionnaires if they are compulsory, otherwise I leave well alone….Other than that, unless it is compulsory I am not prepared to waste my time an that of others by filling in a questionnaire when we do not need "support" in promoting equal opportunities. (The Headteacher's emphasis)

A further, not unconnected reason mentioned was the length and complexity of the questionnaires. As a headteacher, echoing many of his colleagues, commented:

I am afraid that the length and complexity of our questionnaire means that we would have to spend a disproportionate amount of time collecting and completing the information you request.

The questionnaires were designed to yield an array of quantitative data about the situation of schools and LEAs in 1994 by contrast or comparison with the situation in 1984. The aim was to ensure that the data showed the complexities of the changing situation with respect to the characteristics of schools and LEAs and their equal opportunities policies and practices. However, it became clear from the completed questionnaires, and from a number of the non-participants' comments that many schools only kept limited records and could not provide information that went back over a decade.

Another project aim was to elicit a range of perspectives and issues with regard to the educational and social reforms and their relations to gender equality in education. Given the multiplicity of social and educational changes over this ten year period, especially with regard to both the nature and characteristics of schools and education and the curriculum on offer,

181

questions needed to be asked which required careful and perhaps painstaking investigation on the part of schools and LEAs. Again, this proved difficult for many schools which were asked to participate in the project.

A.3 CASE STUDIES OF LEAS AND SCHOOLS

As was mentioned in Chapter 1, the main aim of the case studies was to explore the interconnection between the local context and national policies by way of considering the experience of different local authorities and the range of schools within them. Of particular value was the use of in depth, qualitative methods in order to discover and illustrate the variety of local contexts through which changing national education policy is mediated. Commonalities and differences between schools and LEAs were identified and explored in relation to current provision of equal opportunities. A brief description is given in Chapter 1, of the case studies and the methods of research involved in carrying them out.

The Research Contract

Also mentioned in Chapter 1 is the drawing up of research contracts between LEAs and in some cases, individual schools, which identified the precise relationship between the researchers and the researched, and which also allowed for some negotiation between the two parties where relevant. The research contract (also known as 'Basis of Institutional Collaboration') contained a brief discussion of the aims and the scope of the project, and a description of the research approaches and the forms of data collection envisaged.

It concentrated, in particular, on the different forms of data collection utilised in the case studies, including:

- analysis of school and LEA policies on gender and equal opportunities, historically and currently;

- staff and student/pupil audit;

- review of curriculum policies and practices;

- review of documentation and statistical evidence including 'league tables', SATs results etc.; and

- review of practices pertinent to gender equality issues.

The Research Contract also outlined the variety of anticipated research approaches that would be undertaken within the case studies. These included:

- *Participant Observation* of meetings and interviews related to gender equality issues.

- *Analysis of Documents* of educational policy and structures; publicly available documents such as mission statements, prospectuses, annual reports etc.

- *Interviews* with selected LEA and school personnel.

- *Data Analysis* of student/pupil and staff figures and resource allocations more generally, e.g. for staff development.

Ethical guidelines were offered which involved the project in:

- having reasonable access to relevant documents and meetings but only copying files, correspondence or other internal documents with permission;

- treating all interviews, meetings, oral and written exchanges with participants as 'on the record' unless asked to keep them confidential;

- where practicable, and providing that the permission of participants is given, tape-recording oral data for transcription or summary;

- where practicable, returning written accounts to participants /interviewees who were given a period of twenty-one days to suggest revisions; and

- where feasible, creating computerised systems for database and analysis purposes to which only members of the research team would have access.

Within the Research Contract, research reports were described as containing two main elements: description, and interpretation. Case study institutions were to be provided with fictitious identities and individuals referred to by role-descriptions or pseudonyms. While, it was claimed, these strategies did not guarantee absolute anonymity, they could reduce the possibility of individuals (and institutions) being easily identified.

After discussion and amendments to the contract, institutional representatives were asked to sign the contract as confirmation of agreement to participate in the case study part of the project. Not all schools or LEAs insisted on these formalities, nor did they request such involvement.

APPENDIX B ENTRY AND PERFORMANCE GAPS

TABLE B.1 GCSE entry and performance gap[1]

per cent

	1985	1988	1991	1994
BIOLOGY				
entry gap	-30.09	-28.24	-23.01	-3.21
performance difference	-19.33	-21.16	-16.05	2.34
performance gap	-10.76	-7.09	-6.96	-5.54
CHEMISTRY				
entry gap	15.81	13.85	11.65	21.56
performance difference	19.58	17.58	14.30	20.09
performance gap	-3.77	-3.73	-2.65	1.47
PHYSICS				
entry gap	51.90	47.11	41.40	33.62
performance difference	47.75	43.65	37.27	31.57
performance gap	4.15	3.46	4.13	2.05
SCIENCE				
entry gap	9.55	9.52	5.27	2.51
performance difference	16.15	12.78	7.49	3.86
performance gap	-6.60	-3.27	-2.22	-1.36
MATHS				
entry gap	5.53	0.93	-1.88	-1.53
performance difference	16.89	10.76	1.65	0.32
performance gap	-11.35	-9.83	-3.53	-1.84
COMPUTER STUDIES				
entry gap	36.44	32.99	20.42	29.50
performance difference	47.60	35.81	13.67	24.09
performance gap	-11.17	-2.82	6.75	5.41
CDT				
entry gap	87.06	83.95	64.70	51.10
performance difference	80.77	80.36	57.11	37.81
performance gap	6.29	3.57	7.59	13.29
HOME ECONOMICS				
entry gap	-82.56	-77.34	-75.02	-74.39
performance difference	-91.50	-84.70	-85.32	-84.08
performance gap	8.94	10.36	10.30	11.69
TECHNOLOGY				
entry gap	19.03	18.77	13.40	11.96
performance difference	17.93	13.41	5.95	1.03
performance gap	1.10	5.36	7.45	10.93
GEOGRAPHY				
entry gap	19.00	19.12	15.48	13.63
performance difference	16.94	12.70	10.02	7.32
performance gap	2.07	6.42	5.46	6.31
HISTORY				
entry gap	1.72	0	-2.68	-4.40
performance difference	0.70	-6.46	-7.96	-10.16
performance gap	1.03	6.46	5.28	5.76

TableB.1 contd - GCSE entry and performance gap

	1985	1988	1991	1994
ECONOMICS				
entry gap	4.26	22.83	27.02	32.75
performance difference	5.02	25.45	28.21	32.25
performance gap	-0.77	-2.63	-1.19	0.5
SOCIAL SCIENCES				
entry gap	-18.89	-36.74	-41.74	-42.21
performance difference	-36.81	-51.17	-52.22	-52.69
performance gap	17.92	14.42	10.48	10.48
VOCATIONAL STUDIES				
entry gap	-24.15	-32.91	-36.78	-33.35
performance difference	-19.33	-39.35	-42.51	-42.41
performance gap	-4.82	6.44	5.72	8.86
ART AND DESIGN				
entry gap	-0.84	-5.27	-5.01	-3.71
performance difference	-18.82	-22.19	-20.27	-19.52
performance gap	17.98	16.92	15.26	15.82
ENGLISH				
entry gap	0	0	0	0
performance difference	-12.71	-15.80	-13.27	-13.94
performance gap	12.71	15.80	13.27	13.94
ENGLISH LITERATUE				
entry gap	-13.27	-8.23	-5.71	-5.76
performance difference	-18.61	-19.58	-16.68	-16.29
performance gap	5.36	11.36	10.97	10.53
MFL				
entry gap	-20.29	-18.08	-13.16	-9.48
performance difference	-22.51	-23.24	-21.78	-21.89
performance gap	2.23	5.17	8.62	12.41

[1]

- **Entry gap or performance difference** means a preponderance of female students
(+) **Entry gap or performance difference** means a preponderance of male students

- **Performance gap** indicates higher male success in achieving A-C grades
(+) **Performance gap** indicates higher female success in achieving A-C grades

TABLE B.2   A-Level entry and performance gap[1]

				per cent
	1985	**1988**	**1991**	**1994**
BIOLOGY				
entry gap	-25.52	-24.58	-23.40	-16.13
performance difference	-21.44	-20.00	-20.98	-16.98
performance gap	-4.08	-4.58	-2.43	0.85
CHEMISTRY				
entry gap	21.13	16.38	19.08	19.11
performance difference	28.05	23.77	21.27	21.10
performance gap	-6.91	-7.39	-2.19	-1.99
PHYSICS				
entry gap	54.17	52.32	55.86	60.05
performance difference	59.59	57.15	58.83	59.75
performance gap	-5.42	-4.83	-2.97	0.30
MATHS				
entry gap	36.35	39.79	33.86	34.75
performance difference	40.96	46.16	37.50	35.70
performance gap	-4.61	-6.37	-3.64	-0.95
COMPUTER STUDIES				
entry gap	62.17	69.99	61.99	67.13
performance difference	78.08	83.61	78.51	76.92
performance gap	-15.91	-13.63	-16.53	-9.79
TECHNOLOGY				
entry gap	18.40	34.03	38.06	47.12
performance difference	27.43	41.66	48.88	49.63
performance gap	-9.03	-7.64	-10.82	-2.51
GEOGRAPHY				
entry gap	13.29	13.05	12.83	15.23
performance difference	11.34	11.75	7.49	7.06
performance gap	1.94	1.29	5.33	8.17
HISTORY				
entry gap	-10.12	-10.98	-7.66	-4.12
performance difference	2.43	0.69	-0.71	-0.45
performance gap	-12.55	-11.66	-6.95	-3.66
ECONOMICS				
entry gap	17.52	14.35	25.32	35.84
performance difference	30.20	27.52	32.84	38.46
performance gap	-12.69	-13.17	-7.52	-2.61
SOCIAL STUDIES				
entry gap	-22.30	-28.72	-27.68	-27.11
performance difference	-19.06	-28.35	-23.88	-30.30
performance gap	-3.24	-0.37	-3.80	3.19
ART AND DESIGN				
entry gap	-29.16	-27.79	-24.01	-17.60
performance difference	-25.44	-23.27	-24.85	-22.85
performance gap	-3.72	-4.52	0.84	5.25

187

TableB.2 contd - A-level entry and performance gap

	1985	1988	1991	1994
ENGLISH				
entry gap	-43.65	-42.53	-38.61	-33.87
performance difference	-41.35	-39.83	-33.75	-33.44
performance gap	-2.30	-2.70	-4.86	-0.43
MFL				
entry gap	-46.48	-46.04	-39.90	-33.91
performance difference	-40.81	-38.67	-34.36	-29.04
performance gap	-5.67	-7.37	-5.54	-4.87
CDT				
entry gap	50.61	56.24	70.44	67.68
performance difference	46.73	55.85	72.13	64.26
performance gap	3.88	0.39	-1.69	3.43

[1]

-	**Entry gap or performance difference** means a preponderance of female students
(+)	**Entry gap or performance difference** means a preponderance of male students

-	**Performance gap** indicates higher male success in achieving A-B grades
(+)	**Performance gap** indicates higher female success in achieving A-B grades

BIBLIOGRAPHY

Arnot, M. (1989) 'Consultation or legitimation? Race and gender politics and the making of the national curriculum', **Critical Social Policy** Vol 27, 9, 3 pp. 20-39

Arnot, M. and Weiner, G. (eds.) (1987) **Gender and the Politics of Schooling**. London: Hutchinson

Audit Commission and HMI (1993) **Unfinished Business**. London: Audit Commission

Bailey, V. (1992) Student Non-Completion of BTEC Programmes and Awards. Internal Report, London: BTEC

Burton, L. (ed.) (1986) **Girls into Maths Can Go**. East Sussex: Holt, Rinehart and Winston

Burton, L. and Weiner, G. (1990) 'Social Justice and the National Curriculum', **Research Papers in Education**, 5, 3, pp. 203-228

Central Statistical Office (1993) **Social Trends**. London: HMSO

Central Statistical Office (1994) **Social Trends**. London: HMSO

Chisholm, L. and Holland, J. (1986) 'Girls and Occupational Choice: Anti-sexism in action in a curriculum development project', **British Journal of Sociology of Education**, 7, 4

Clarricoates, K. (1978) 'Dinosaurs in the classroom - a re-examination of some aspects of the "hidden curriculum" in primary schools', **Women's Studies International Quarterly**, 1, pp. 353-64

David, M.E. (1980) **The State, the Family and Education**. London: Routledge and Kegan Paul

David, M.E. (1993) **Parents, Gender and Education Reform**. Cambridge: Polity Press

Department for Education (1994a) **Statistical Bulletin**. 1/94

Department for Education (1994b) **Statistics of Education**. London: HMSO

Department for Education (1995) **Statistics of Education**. London: HMSO

Department for Education, Welsh Office, Scottish Office Education Department, Department of Education for Northern Ireland and the University Funding Council (1992) **Education Statistics for the United Kingdom**. London: HMSO

Department for Education, Welsh Office, Scottish Office Education Department, Department of Education for Northern Ireland and the University Funding Council (1993) **Education Statistics for the United Kingdom**. London: HMSO

Equal Opportunities Commission (1988) 'An unpublished EOC survey of Local Education Authorities'. Manchester: EOC

Equal Opportunities Commission (1994) **Response to National Education and Training Targets**. Manchester: EOC

Felstead, A. Goodwin, J. and Green, F. (1995) **Measuring up to the National Training Targets: Women's Attainment of Vocational Qualifications**. Research Report, Centre for Labour Market Studies: University of Leicester

Gipps, C. and Murphy, P. (1994) **A Fair Test? Assessment, Achievement and Equity**. Buckingham: Open University Press

Inner London Education Authority (1986a) **Primary Matters**. London: ILEA

Inner London Education Authority (1986b) **Secondary Issues**. London: ILEA

Kelly, A. (1985) 'Changing schools and changing society: some reflections on the Girls into Science and Technology project', in Arnot, M. (ed.) **Race and Gender: equal opportunities policies in education**. Oxford: Pergamon

Lees, S. (1987) 'The structure of sexual relations in school', in Arnot, M. and Weiner, G. (eds.) **Gender and the Politics of Schooling**. London: Hutchinson

Maccoby, E.E. and Jacklin, C.N. (1974) **The Psychology of Sex Differences**. London: Oxford University Press

Manpower Services Commission (1984) **TVEI: Annual Review.** London: MSC

McIntyre, T. (1987) **Equal Opportunities for Boys and Girls in TVEI: An evaluation progress report.** Sheffield: TVEI

Miles, S. and Middleton, C. (1990) 'Girls' Education in the Balance: the ERA and Inequality', in Flude, M. and Hammer, M. (eds.) **The Education Reform Act 1988: Its Origins and Implications**. Basingstoke: Falmer Press

Millman, V. (1987) 'Teacher as researcher: a new tradition for research on gender', in Weiner, G. and Arnot, M. (eds.) **Gender Under Scrutiny**. London: Hutchinson

Millman, V. and Weiner, G. (1985) **Sex Differentiation in Schools: is there really a problem?**. York: Longman

Moon, B. (1994) **A Guide to the National Curriculum**, 2nd edition. Oxford: Oxford University Press

Myers, K. (1986) **Genderwatch**. London: SCDC (revised and reprinted in 1992, Cambridge: Cambridge University Press)

National Advisory Council for Education and Training Targets (1994) **Report on Progress**. London: NACETT

National Advisory Council for Education and Training Targets (1995) **Developing Skills for a Successful Future.** London: NACETT

National Council for Vocational Qualifications (1991) **The NVQ Framework**. London: NCVQ

National Foundation of Educational Research (1993) **TVEI Briefing No. 3: Towards equality of opportunity.** Slough: NFER

Office of Standards of Education (1993a) **Boys and English**. London: Department for Education

Office of Standards of Education (1993b) **Framework for the Inspection of Schools**. London: OFSTED

Orr, P. (1984) 'Sex bias in schools: national perspectives', in Whyte, J., Deem, R., Kant, L. and Cruickshank, M. (eds.) **Girl Friendly Schooling**. London: Methuen

Pratt, J., Bloomfield, J., and Seale, C. (1984) **Option Choice: A Question of Equal Opportunity**. Slough: NFER-Nelson

Riley, K. (1994) **Quality and Equality: promoting opportunities in schools**. London: Cassell

Runnymede Trust (1993) **Equality Assurance in Schools: Quality, Identity, Society**. London: Trentham Books

Salisbury, J. (1996) **Educational Reforms and Gender Equality in Welsh Schools**. Cardiff: EOC

School Curriculum and Assessment Authority (1993) **The National Curriculum and its Assessment - Final Report (The Dearing Report)**. London: SCAA

School Curriculum and Assessment Authority (1994a) **Report on the 1994 Key Stage 1 Tests and Tasks in English and Mathematics**, ref. KS1/94/128. London: SCAA

School Curriculum and Assessment Authority/Curriculum and Assessment Authority for Wales (1994b) **Report on 1994 Key Stage 2 Pilot**, ref. KS2/94/129. London: SCAA

School Curriculum and Assessment Authority (1994c) **Report on the 1994 Key Stage 3 Tests and Tasks in English**, ref. KS3/94/119. London: SCAA

School Curriculum and Assessment Authority (1994d) **Report on the 1994 Key Stage 3 Tests and Tasks in Mathematics**, ref. KS3/94/120. London: SCAA

School Curriculum and Assessment Authority (1994e) **Report on the 1994 Key Stage 3 Tests and Tasks in Science**, ref. KS3/94/121. London: SCAA

Shah, S. (1990) 'Equal Opportunity Issues in the Context of the National Curriculum: a Black perspective', **Gender and Education**, 2 (3), pp. 309-318

Spender, D. (1980) **Man Made Language**. London: Routledge and Kegan Paul

Stobart, G., White, J., Elwood, J., Hayden, M. and Mason, K. (1992) 'Differential Performance at 16+: English and Mathematics'. London: SEAC

Surrey County Council (1994) **Evaluation of the Impact of Pre-school Experience on Year R Screening**. County Director of Education Report: Surrey County Council

Tarsh, J., Sanders, N., and Reed, R. (1994) **Science and Maths: a Consultation Paper on the Supply and Demand of Newly Qualified People**. London: Department for Education

TVEI (1991) **Equality of Opportunity? Managing Educational Entitlement**. Sheffield: TVEI

Weiner, G. (1994) **Feminisms in Education: an introduction**. Buckingham: Open University Press

Weiner, G., and Arnot, M. (1987) 'Teachers and gender politics', in Arnot, M. and Weiner, G. (eds.) **Gender and the Politics of Schooling**. London: Hutchinson.

Whitty, G. (1989) 'Central Control or Market Forces', in Flude, M. and Hammer, M. (eds.) **The Education Reform Act 1988: its Origins and Implications**. Basingstoke: Faber Press

Whyld, J. (1983) **Sexism in the Secondary Curriculum**. London: Harper and Row

Whyte, J. (1983) **Beyond the Wendy House: Sex Role Stereotyping in Primary Schools**. York: Longman

Whyte, J., Deem, R., Kant, L. and Cruickshank, M. (eds.) (1984) **Girl Friendly Schooling**. London: Methuen

Wright, C. (1987) 'The relations between teachers and Afro-Caribbean pupils: observing multiracial classrooms', in Weiner, G. and Arnot, M. (eds.) **Gender Under Scrutiny** London: Hutchinson